Becoming
a Healthy Church

Workbook

Becoming
a Healthy Church
Workbook

Stephen A. Macchia

Baker Books

A Division of Baker Book House Co
Grand Rapids, Michigan 49516

© 2001 by Stephen A. Macchia

Published by Baker Books
a division of Baker Book House Company
P.O. Box 6287, Grand Rapids, MI 49516-6287

Printed in the United States of America

ISBN 0-8010-9118-7

For current information about all releases from Baker Book House, visit our web site:
http://www.bakerbooks.com

This workbook is dedicated to every church bold enough to bring discipline into their life together so that genuinely healthy spiritual renewal can emerge through discovering, celebrating, and recognizing God's unique thumbprint on their life together in ministry.

And to the entire Vision New England Team, for the incredible way they balance their roles as humble servants and strategic leaders for the body of Christ in New England.

Contents

A Distinctive Approach

Becoming a Healthy Church Workbook guides the pastor and leadership team through a process of dialogue, assessment, and planning that is:

Spirit-led—relying on the wisdom of God as discerned by people of prayer and the Word of God

Principle-based—enhancing a philosophy of ministry with the Ten Characteristics of a Healthy Church as the foundation

User-friendly—readily usable materials that allow the team to begin the process immediately and without waiting for additional training

Team-focused—listening to one another and developing plans for future ministry in the context of the body of Christ

Cost-efficient—affordable workbook and ancillary support materials

Tailor-made—questions that allow the church to discover its unique, God-given thumbprint

Long-lasting—timeless resources and a manageable process that's doable, not only initially but on an annual basis

Locally owned—implementation of decisions allows for ongoing development of ministry within the context of the local church setting

Results-oriented—purposeful goals and action steps, articulated in language that encourages life-changing transformation

All-inclusive—all areas of local church life are explored in depth, and, as a result, all ministry initiatives are enhanced, building on their strengths and celebrating what God is already doing in the midst of his people

Acknowledgments

This workbook was a team effort. When the characteristics of a healthy church were first developed, a team was put in place to begin the process of sharing this material with church leaders, urging them to use the Ten Characteristics of a Healthy Church as a benchmark for their local church's evaluation. Mark MacDonald, Dennis Baril, David Midwood, and Kim Strepka were diligent at the early stages of development.

The next generation of leaders who were added to the team included Bob Ludwig, Pat McGowan, and a team of facilitators who tested this concept in several local church settings. My faithful assistant, Carole Nason, is the primary Bible student who compiled the Scriptures on Jesus and the Ten Characteristics of a Healthy Church. David Midwood created the helpful appendix of sermon outlines on the ten characteristics.

I am especially grateful to Bob Ludwig for his support of all of our healthy church initiatives and for providing the case study from a local church facilitation he conducted. All along the way, the entire staff team at Vision New England participated at various levels in disseminating this material far and wide. In addition, our Board of Directors, led so capably by Caleb Loring, urged us forward in these initiatives, believing wholeheartedly in their importance.

Finally, and most significantly, my family stood by on the sidelines cheering me on with love and encouragement. My deepest gratitude is extended to my precious wife, Ruth, and our delightful children, Nathan and Rebekah.

To God be the glory. Great things he has done!

About the Workbook

What will it take for your church to become a healthier church? Given the realities of your particular ministry setting, how will you begin that process? If you were to start that process today, what would it look like? Who would be included? What topics and issues would you explore? How would you define your anticipated results for the near and distant future?

These are the kinds of questions effective leaders in the church of Jesus Christ are asking themselves today. And these are the questions that will be explored in this workbook, the companion volume to *Becoming a Healthy Church* (Baker, 1999).

For more than two decades now, I have observed many leadership teams wrestle with strategic issues and ideas in an exhilarating manner. Leaders love to talk about the latest trends affecting ministry today. They enjoy discussing what others seem to be discovering and implementing in other local church settings. The disconnect comes when they start looking at their respective settings and determine which of the brightest and best ideas "out there" have application back on the home front.

When leadership teams select from the menu of offerings "out there" without first looking at "what's here," they in essence abort the planning process without really getting started. It's great for you to learn about how others are leading their churches, what principles are guiding their thought processes, and what programs are emerging for ministry. But when you do that to the exclusion of first searching for God's unique agenda for your church, you are limiting what he has in mind for you and your congregation.

Discover Your Thumbprint

Every local church has a unique thumbprint given to them by God. In your pursuit of church health and vitality, there needs to be a discovery process that uncovers that uniqueness. When it's discerned, there needs to be a celebration of those distinctives. In response, there arise plans, programs, and ministry opportunities that express the unique persona of your people.

Imagine for a moment that there were no resources available to you for the purpose of "cloning" programs from church A back into your church. What if you were to wipe your library clean of every available resource that serves as a how-to guide for doing every imaginable area of ministry? Could you survive for a month or a year without attending another conference and collecting yet another new training manual for your already loaded shelves?

What do you think would happen if you could literally stop the conveyor belt of ideas from infiltrating your mailbox and cluttering your mind with every conceivable ministry's latest and greatest ideas for you to buy and implement in your local church? What if you chose right now, today in fact, to say no to another appointment with someone outside of your local ministry setting who needs "just a few minutes of your time" to share his or her latest ministry resource with you? Is it possible for you to hop off your treadmill for just a few months to assess your current state of church health without considering anyone else's ideas for how *you* should be leading your church into greater health and vitality?

I guarantee (for whatever my guarantee is worth!) that if you step away from the incredible demands that are biting at your ankles each day and start asking the hard questions about your uniquely God-ordained thumbprint, your ministry will never be the same again. That's right, *never* be the same again.

Weigh In, Please!

The last time I went to my doctor for my annual physical, the nurse greeted me with a smile and politely invited me to "weigh in, please!" I thought to myself, *She is just too perky for me today.* Frankly the last thing I wanted to do at that moment was to divulge something as personal as my weight to a complete stranger. I reluctantly stepped on the scale (after first taking off my shoes, watch, sport coat, and tie and removing the wallet from my back pants pocket.) and "weighed in." The only consolation was the fact that the nurse was indeed a complete stranger, unable to share such confidential information with anyone else but my doctor.

It's not that I'm such an overweight person, despite what I feel about myself. It's just that "weighing in" was the opening exercise of that less-than-pleasant annual drill of activities at my doctor's office, and I wasn't thrilled about it. But through the weighing-in procedure, I began the process of unveiling (literally) the true picture of my current physical state. The doctor needed this picture before he could tell me how to become a healthier person.

At the end of the visit to my doctor, I had confidence that I had been inspected from head to toe by an expert in his field. He gave me encouraging news about my physical condition and he made specific suggestions about follow-up tests he wanted me to take, a new medication he chose to prescribe, and another specialist he recommended that I see for a particular need. He didn't point at pictures of other people he wished I looked like and he didn't compare me with other patients with different ailments. He focused on me and my reality and with great empathy made some excellent suggestions for me to follow.

I followed his advice to the letter. As a result, I am feeling better than ever, with renewed energy for the days ahead. I was invigorated by the visit and what my doctor had to say. Even though it complicates life a bit with some of my new discoveries and restrictions, I feel prepared to face the days ahead with a remarkable zest for life.

My hope is that, in a similar manner, by following the exercises in this workbook, you will feel much better about your church! You and your team will define your present realities, while coming up with prescriptive measures best suited for your unique design as a church. You will explore topics that are relevant to your current ministry context, all the while sorting out priorities for the months and years ahead. The process will be exhilarating if you are willing to take that first step and "weigh in!"

Diagnosis/Prognosis

Weighing in is just the first step in the process. If you recall from your own annual physicals, there are also the blood pressure and temperature checks, blood and urine tests, and a multiplicity of other routine exam procedures designed to proactively address any apparent or potential physical concerns. It's far better to be ahead of the curve on such matters than to have to react to crises and emergencies.

We've become very familiar with doctors' offices over the years. Our son Nathan (whom I told you about in *Becoming a Healthy Church*) has been to Children's Hospital in Boston dozens of times over the past several years. He routinely is being checked out regarding his unique condition that has evidenced itself in a weak and sickly tibia in his right leg. The orthopedic surgeons have been wonderful for Nathan, not only diagnosing his illness but providing prognoses for his future that offer hope and promise—despite his significant health challenges.

There is a huge difference between diagnosis and prognosis. Diagnosis is defined as "the act or process of deciding the nature of a diseased condition by examination of the symptoms; a careful examination and analysis of the facts in an attempt to understand or explain something." Whereas prognosis is "a forecast or prediction of the probable course of a disease and the chances of recovery for that individual." Diagnosis focuses on the present facts while prognosis provides information about the future.

In southern Connecticut, along one of the major interstate highways, there are three wonderful billboards for a local hospital that express the difference between these two terms. On one of these billboards, there is the face of a young child, a girl, probably close to ten years old.

Underneath her face are the words: "Diagnosis—asthma. Prognosis—runs the Boston Marathon." A second billboard a few miles away has a face of an older man, most likely in his mid to late sixties. The caption under his picture reads: "Diagnosis—heart condition. Prognosis—roller-coaster enthusiast." Farther up the road is a third billboard with the face of a young woman, in her mid to late twenties. Her caption reads: "Diagnosis—cancer. Prognosis—grandmother."

These billboards not only describe the difference between diagnosis and prognosis, but they give *hope* to each patient depicted. Regardless of the condition of the debilitating disease, the prognosis for their futures is hope-filled. By going to the medical center being advertised on the billboards, you not only receive treatment for your diagnosed ailments, you also are given some hope for your future. Even if the diagnosis is devastating, the medical personnel are committed to helping their patients see a prognosis that includes some sense of hope.

And so it is with your church. Regardless of the current health condition—the diagnosis—of your local church, a healthy prognosis for your future that's filled to the brim and overflowing with hope will give your congregation renewed energy for the future.

A Holy Spirit–directed process of discovering God's unique thumbprint for your church must include hope for tomorrow. He is the Great Physician in this process, overseeing your health checkup with his eyes, ears, and heart wide open to your needs and aspirations. He will not leave you or forsake you throughout this process. He will hold you securely in the palms of his hands as he leads you every step of the way. By his strong, guiding hand, the journey will be made all the richer. Trust him for a hope-filled prognosis, even when the diagnostic elements of dialogue and assessment become tiresome in unpackaging the truest picture of your current reality.

The Process

Once you have decided to jump into the process of discovering God's unique thumbprint for your church, you will need to be cheered on to victory. I wish I could be there for you as you begin this process with your leadership team and congregation. If I were there, I would remind you of several important ingredients to the experience you are about to share.

A Long-Term Process

Please remember all along the way that discovering God's unique thumbprint for your church is long term. You will work at it intensively for the first four to six months, but it doesn't end there. The initial stages of this discovery process are critical to the success of the total experience but do not constitute the sum total of the process. What's essential for every leader involved is to embrace the magnitude of the process with growing excitement for the results that will be experienced all along the way. Don't let any seeds of discouragement, disappointment, or discord be planted in the hearts and minds of the key leaders involved. Even though the process is long term, it is also very:

- joy-filled
- faith-based
- vision-focused
- team-centered
- Christ-honoring
- Spirit-led

A Committed Team

The more your team is involved in the journey of discovery, the more you will ultimately get out of this process. The more they own the process, the greater the impact will be as a result. Choose together to *stop* (at least for the time being) looking over your shoulder at other, more successful churches and look instead to God for his design for your local church. As a result, find freedom in Christ to be and become all he intends for you in the fulfillment of his thumbprint within your church.

A Discerning Leader

After you discover your unique gifts and abilities as a congregation, the time will come to turn to those bookshelves, attend those conferences, consider those ministry experts, and consult those training manuals but, this time, with the realization that every "good idea" coming down the pike will not necessarily be the best idea for you and your local church. Become a discerning leader; pick and choose what fits best for your ministry today and what will be most needed for the future. Don't assume that every resource will work until you first attempt to identify your greatest needs and priorities. Then choose resources that fit the bill for meeting these needs and solidifying these priorities so that your ministry effectiveness quotient increases significantly in the months ahead.

The Goal

All along the way, keep your goal in mind. As you undertake the activities and exercises included in this workbook, remember that the intended result is to become a healthier church! What is a healthy church?

A healthy church is prayerful in all of the following aspects of church life and ministry, is reliant on God's power and the authority of his Word, and values:

1. God's empowering presence
2. God-exalting worship
3. Spiritual disciplines
4. Learning and growing in community
5. A commitment to loving and caring relationships
6. Servant-leadership development
7. An outward focus
8. Wise administration and accountability
9. Networking with the body of Christ
10. Stewardship and generosity

To achieve these objectives, let me exegete for you the full title of this workbook, for every word used has significance for your process.

Becoming a Healthy Church Workbook
A Leadership Team Dialogue, Assessment, and Planning Tool

Becoming a Healthy Church. The obvious goal.

Workbook. This text requires time and effort on your part as pastor and leadership team members. It's a very active process, demanding discipline and participation every step of the way. This interactive process will assist you in moving through a healthy church checkup to a ministry prescription for your future. It will be well worth your investment.

Leadership. This process demands the best of local church leadership teams, in spite of how you may be structured. Intentional direction, prayerful dependence, and visionary service are the elements needed by the team charged with leading the way. This experience will bring out the best in your leaders.

Team. The suggested activities included here must be done in community. Even though many times you will be asked to answer and evaluate from your personal perspective, it will be in the collection of many ideas that you will discern the heart and mind of God. Your team will be invigorated by the process.

Dialogue. Communication is a two-way street. Learning how to effectively listen to one another, reflect on what you hear from each member, and empathize with where others are coming from are all a part of community-building dialogue. When the communication process breaks down and conflict emerges (which is inevitable if you are truly honest with one another!), it's incumbent on the leaders to rise to the occasion and serve as facilitators of Christ-honoring conflict resolution. (See Guidelines on Conflict Resolution on page 27 of this workbook for additional help.) Welcome every comment.

Assessment. Assessment begins with "weighing in" and grows from that point into multiple layers of constructive collaboration on the true picture of your church's current realities. Learning how to ask the right questions, listening for honest feedback, and discerning the current temperature of spirituality in your congregation are essential to determining future direction for ministry. Don't give up midstream—it's worth the effort.

Planning. Ministry plans that grow out of the previous stages of dialogue and assessment will focus on maximizing your strengths and opportunities without being weighed down by your weaknesses and obstacles for service. Strategic initiatives that make good sense to pursue will emerge naturally and will clearly embody the renewing work of the Spirit within your fellowship. A healthy dialogue and assessment process plus the Holy Spirit's direction equals great strategic planning for local churches.

Tool. As you are probably aware, this workbook is but one tool in your ministry toolbox today. The nice thing about this tool is that it's not tied to any one program or set of ministry ideas that others have propagated from one setting to the next, assuming they will work if implemented in the same manner. No, this tool is specifically designed to flow naturally into a variety of selected ministry methods, such as your prescribed denominational programs. In addition, if you are a church that has used programs from Willow Creek (seeker-sensitive model) or Saddleback (purpose-driven model) or New Life Church (life-giving model) or any of a number of large churches involved in leadership training, this tool complements all of those programs. If you begin with this approach first, you will be better prepared to select the methods and programs that would best accentuate your church's unique thumbprint.

My jaw dropped when I received a most encouraging e-mail from Rick Warren, pastor of Saddleback Community Church and author of *Purpose-Driven Church*. He wrote, "I loved reading *Becoming a Healthy Church*. It's a wonderful tool that I recommend to every church that is serious about becoming purpose-driven." Then he proceeded to outline how the Ten Characteristics of a Healthy Church fit perfectly into the purpose-driven model. Rick correlated them as follows (Warren's model is in italics; Ten Characteristics of a Healthy Church are bulleted points):

Worship (Magnification)
- God's Empowering Presence (characteristic 1)
- God-Exalting Worship (characteristic 2)

Discipleship (Maturity)
- Spiritual Disciplines (characteristic 3)
- Learning and Growing in Community (characteristic 4)

Fellowship (Membership)
- A Commitment to Loving and Caring Relationships (characteristic 5)
- Networking with the Body of Christ (characteristic 9)

Service (Ministry)
- Servant-Leadership Development (characteristic 6)
- Wise Administration and Accountability (characteristic 8)

Evangelism (Missions)
- An Outward Focus (characteristic 7)
- Stewardship and Generosity (characteristic 10)

Rick Warren's integration of our work with his was an incredible gift from God and affirmed the fact that the Ten Characteristics of a Healthy Church are a great place to begin before settling into a methodology or specific programs that best articulate your unique passion and mission. It became even more obvious to our team that God was in the midst of our work, and we return all the glory to him.

The Package

In this workbook you will find a treasure chest of resources. There is no way you will use it all! My hope is that you will find the general outline, as seen in the table of contents, clear enough to lead you through this endeavor. Feel free to tailor the material for your specific purposes, maximizing this experience. Find freedom in Christ to pursue the process with your fellow teammates in a way that reflects your personality as a local church. Don't bite off so much that you end up with indigestion as a result!

This workbook is a part of a much larger package of resources for local church leaders interested in becoming a healthier church. Please see appendix D for a list of these resources and ordering information.

Becoming a Healthy Church, published by Baker Book House, is now available in English, Korean, and Russian, with a Spanish version forthcoming. This is the primary text, recommended reading (by at least one member of the leadership team) prior to beginning to use this workbook.

Don't put off your healthy church checkup any longer. Schedule this process into your calendar today and treat it as the most important initiative you will experience in the upcoming months.

This is all part of God's uniquely wonderful strategic plan yet to unfold before your very eyes! Let the journey begin . . .

Heavenly Father, you are the Lord of our local church, the Creator of the ends of the earth, and the lover of our souls. Unite us in this process, we pray. May the early stages of our dialogue and assessment be honoring and pleasing to you. May the quality of our relationships be strengthened in the process. May we find our greatest joy and hope in you as you direct this journey. We love and trust you as our loving God and reigning King. Empower us by your Spirit and give to us hearts like Jesus as we embark on this experience together. We commit ourselves and one another into your loving care, with hearts of gratitude and grace. Lead on O King Eternal! In the name of your Son, our Savior, Jesus Christ, we pray this day. Amen.

Part 1

Let's Get Started

How Do We Know If We're Healthy?

Our lives are a picture of the body of Christ. "All of us in the body walk with a limp of some sort. Our goal in life is not perfection—we are not perfect beings, nor is the church a perfected entity. We are all works in progress, and we are all dependent on God to give us the courage to face each new day of our life and ministry. We will encounter our own shortcomings for the rest of our lives until the Lord returns to usher us into a perfected glory in heaven. In the meantime, we need to assist one another in the process of becoming a healthy church—the pursuit of health and vitality, regardless of the limiting conditions of our lives" (from *Becoming a Healthy Church*, p. 215).

Becoming a Healthy Church grew out of my heart's desire to identify and articulate principles that churches could apply in seeking to become stronger, healthier expressions of the body of Christ in their own community. This tool is designed to help the pastor and church governing board assess the health of their church, realize its God-given potential, and unify the church with a plan that moves toward greater health and vitality. We have already seen this happen in a number of ministry settings when leaders used the contents of this workbook, in its prepublication editions, in the life of their church. Leadership teams that have utilized this format have found that it stimulated some of the best discussions and planning sessions they have ever had as a leadership team.

Here are what some pastors have to say about this process:

"The discussion process educated us on what a church ought to be. It encouraged us to learn what a healthy church looks like and is expanding our vision."—Michael John, Market Street Baptist Church, Amesbury, Massachusetts

"The healthy church assessment process gave us hope when we were feeling that we had no future. Now we know we have a future. We have now had our first person come to personal salvation and have had 85 percent of our people join midweek Bible studies in small groups. To my delight one of the members of a small group has now asked if she could start a children's church ministry!"—Pat Bona, Church of God, Manchester, New Hampshire

"The discussion tool gave us a greater depth of understanding about what we are trying to do and how to do it. It helped us look at our ministries in a more strategic way. We are now going through these questions as staff and the process is helping facilitate team building. We are learning to offer feedback to each other in a helpful way. And the process is actually bringing up a lot more questions than answers, which is good."—Bret Tye, Pine Knolls Alliance Church, South Glens Falls, New York

I strongly believe that all churches should engage in a process of dialogue and assessment each year, or at minimum, every two years. This allows governing boards and congregational members to embark on a healthy communication cycle, which continuously provides feedback loops within the fellowship. As you discipline yourself to becoming good listeners—to the Lord and to one another—these self-assessing healthy church checkups will lead you forward in a very positive way.

The prophet Isaiah describes God's people as "oaks of righteousness, a planting of the LORD for the display of his splendor" (Isa. 61:3). Pursuing the Ten Characteristics of a Healthy Church will assist you in the process of becoming an oak of righteousness. In order for you to become mighty oaks, you need to be open and willing to be transformed—yes, changed—by God so that you can grow to become more like him. He is the Mighty Oak of the universe and we are his acorns, destined for his purposes to be planted near his trunk, interlocking with his lovingly tender roots, growing under the shadow of his protective covering, displaying his splendor, and multiplying ourselves for his glory!

For you to embrace a season of growth and change as an oak of righteousness, there are four "tions" that you dare not shun in the process:

First of all, *reflection*, which is the discipline that takes you off the treadmill of ministry activity and into a time of listening, first to God and then to one another. Reflection allows you time to hear how the story of God's kingdom has emerged over time in the fellowship of your church.

Second, *affirmation*, which is the intentional attitude of gratitude for all that God has done well in your midst over the years. It's here that you thank God for the "good work he has begun" in you and through you and to those outside the faith that you have been called to serve.

Third, *evaluation*, which is the constructive commentary of how effective or how inadequate your ministry efforts have been over the past year(s). Healthy evaluation is spoken and received in the spirit of love, with a heart to restore, renew, and reinvigorate the work of God in your midst.

Fourth, *application*, where the conversations about the past cease and the planning for an exciting future begins. If the first three "tions" are completed without application, then the dialogue process is limited or reduced to an inward, "navel gazing" experience only and does not set you free to become all that God intends!

If you as a leader are willing to embrace the disciplines, as described above, in assessing yourself, you will be far more open to lead others in this process. I have discovered the pure joy of ongoing assessment that has led to incredible growth and maturity—for me personally and for my colleagues who have embraced its importance as well. It's not something to be shunned but welcomed. The growth you will experience will aid you in becoming all that God intends.

When you embrace the disciplines of reflection, affirmation, evaluation, and application, then you are heading in the right direction for a meaningful assessment experience and growth as a healthy church. There are several advantages for taking this course of action, including the following:

1. Healthy churches are more biblical and pursue God's design for their ministry together—even when it requires changes along the way.
2. Healthy churches are more evangelistic and open to new ways of reaching this generation with the gospel of Jesus Christ.
3. Healthy churches are more effective in helping Christians grow and are willing to evaluate how helpful each program is for all members.
4. Healthy churches are more prayerful and therefore are wide open to hear from the Holy Spirit for his direction for their worship, fellowship, discipleship, and witness.

You could manufacture your own assessment process and utilize it in the life of your church, or you can use the tried-and-tested one provided for you here! It's that simple. However, there may be people in your church who are confused by the need for an "organized" process as opposed to "just getting together and giving us an opportunity to vent our feelings about the church." It's precisely for that reason—and many more reasons—that such a process is most productive when it's organized and led appropriately.

When people ask why an organized assessment process is best, I explain to them the following points:

1. The process provides structure—a beginning, an end, and helpful tools for meaningful dialogue and strategic planning that's user-friendly for your congregation.
2. The process affirms all the things that are currently being done well, celebrating the work of God already in your midst.
3. The process channels constructive criticism in a positive manner, so that the naysayers don't rule the day!
4. The process encourages an annual comparison, looking back on the prior year's

accomplishments as you look ahead for what's in store in the months ahead.

5. The process tracks your improvements along the way, giving ongoing opportunity to rejoice together in the forward motion being experienced in your context of ministry.

6. The process provides assistance to the pastor and leadership team, so that the plans that are constructed for the future are not made in a vacuum.

7. The process allows plenty of flexibility for different churches, recognizing the distinct elements of church life and governmental polity in diverse ministry settings.

8. The process tends to defuse long-term buildup of conflict, allowing opportunity for your members to offer both affirmation and concern in their communication.

9. The process helps the leaders develop ministry plans in line with God's priorities for the church instead of leaning on their own wisdom.

10. The process makes it safe for people to speak up and express their opinions, feelings, and ideas, recognizing that no idea or comment is off-limits (unless it's presented to be counterproductive to the process for one reason or another).

It's vitally important that leadership step to the plate and take charge of this process so that any number of potential pitfalls can be avoided. One potential pitfall is getting caught up on one or two "hot topics" and being stuck there, unable to move forward because of the enormity of the topic or because one or two dominant people try to control the process. Also, this process can cause old conflicts to reemerge, and these need to be dealt with appropriately without bogging down the whole process. In addition, you can allow the process to get too complex, inviting too many questions and comments that end up derailing the dialogue and frustrating your members. If the process is too elongated, if unclear directions or unrealistic expectations are set up, these too can hinder your effectiveness. Pitfalls like these are for avoiding—as proactively as possible!

The fact of the matter is your members are assessing your church every Sunday. An organized process harnesses that assessment in a productive fashion, one that honors the Lord and shows respect for each leader and each member of the congregation.

Guidelines for Leaders on Facilitating Effective Dialogue

The purpose of dialogue is to seek mutual understanding and harmony. In essence, it's the process of building healthy, successful relationships. Dialogue builds community and a common sense of mission and purpose. It breaks down barriers and builds strength within the team and the broader family.

Effective dialogue encourages you to grow in love for one another. That alone is a good enough reason for meaningful engagement in the process. In dialogue everyone coming to the table shares an equal role in the discussion; no grandstanding is allowed! Listening with empathy—willing to walk in one another's moccasins—is a must. Dialogue also brings out assumptions that otherwise would lie dormant in your church.

In his book *The Magic of Dialogue* (Simon and Schuster, 1999, pages 129–46), author Daniel Yankelovich describes the ten potholes to avoid in overcoming the challenges of dialogue. They are:

holding back—being reluctant to participate

being locked into a box—unable to think beyond the status quo

prematurely moving to action—the tendency to rush into action

listening without hearing—the unwillingness to empathetically understand

starting at different points—members at different stages of the judgment curve on an issue

showboating—showing off how much we know about the subject

scoring debate points—listening only to offer a competitive response

contrarianism—automatically advancing an opposite opinion to set off fireworks

having a pet preoccupation—being obsessed with a single idea or interest

aria singing—unable to resist the temptation to advance a special interest, however ill-timed.

When effectively acknowledged by the facilitator and recognized by the group, these potholes can be avoided. If allowed to persist, they can kill dialogue and ultimately destroy the process. The goal is to set up a system for effective dialogue that cuts through the barriers and achieves tremendous results. I hope that you will find the system suggested in this workbook to be helpful to your process.

Organization of the Assessment Tool

The main body of the dialogue and assessment tool follows a format that is designed to make it as user-friendly as possible. Each of the Ten Characteristics of a Healthy Church is addressed in a separate section, which contains the following:

- An abbreviated overview of the characteristic
- Several key points that describe the characteristic
- Several Scriptures that give Jesus' teachings on the characteristic
- The key points along with a scale of 1 to 10, allowing assessors to rank the effectiveness of the congregation on each point
- A space for personal notes, to retain the reasons behind the rating
- An overall rating for the characteristic on a scale of 1 to 10
- Three concluding open-ended questions:

1. What are we doing to live out this characteristic today?
2. Where do we want to be in this characteristic one or two years from now?
3. How will we get where we want to be in living out this characteristic in the next year or two?

Before people in the congregation and/or on the leadership team are asked to complete their own assessment of the church using the contents of this workbook, the leader of the process may wish to assign background material to help each person think through the issues about to be raised. It is helpful if as many involved in the process as possible read *Becoming a Healthy Church*, or, at minimum, study together the basic outline of the Ten Characteristics of a Healthy Church, found in the booklet "Ten Characteristics of a Healthy Church," available from Vision New England. (See appendix D for ordering information.) In addition, the appendixes of this workbook are designed to provide helpful materials to enhance this dialogue and assessment experience.

Few churches will take full advantage of all the resources available in this workbook and through Vision New England, but as you revisit this process on an annual basis, these additional resources will help to keep this process fresh and invigorating for all who are involved in the strategic dialogue, assessment, and planning work of the church.

Questions to Answer

In planning a church assessment, there are several questions that must be answered.

First of all, who should lead the dialogue and assessment process?

I would suggest that the leader be the pastor, an outside trained facilitator, or the pastor and a trusted layperson who has good group dynamics skills.

Whoever is assigned to lead the dialogue and assessment experience needs to be skilled as a facilitator. A facilitator is distinctly different from a consultant. A consultant comes into a setting to perform independent research and then offer advice to the pastor and/or leadership board. A facilitator guides an "in-house" group in the process of reaching their own conclusions. Strictly speaking, a facilitator does not do research on his or her own and does not expect that his or her advice will be the only grist for the mill of dialogue, assessment, and planning.

There are several issues surrounding the topic of effective facilitation that must be considered before a person is identified and chosen for this role. The following is a listing of characteristics and guidelines for an effective facilitator, gleaned partially from *The Art of Facilitation* by Dale Hunter, Anne Bailey, and Bill Taylor (Tucson: Fisher Books, 1995, pp. 31–46).

A good facilitator:

- Is aware of his or her own strengths and weaknesses
- Is aware of his or her biases in a given situation
- Believes there is synergy in group dynamics
- Is a good listener
- Does not think there is one right way to do most things
- Can be empathetic
- Can admit when he or she doesn't understand
- Enjoys being with people
- Reads body language well
- Is highly intuitive and picks up on the emotional climate of the group

An effective facilitator will do the following:

- Review the self-assessment process from start to finish
- Encourage each group member to participate
- Make it safe for divergent views to be expressed (no ideas are bad ideas)
- Keep the group on track (know what you need to achieve in a given meeting)
- Be flexible—accept a different approach when appropriate
- Be yourself—let your own personality show through

- Listen for what is not said (what is being avoided?)
- Summarize and repeat back to the group comments that are made
- Read body language and watch for who isn't participating
- Ask lots of questions
- Use humor when appropriate
- Build consensus in the areas of agreement
- Celebrate areas of agreement as success

Second, what church group organizes and takes the lead in the assessment?

The most appropriate options are the pastor and key governing board, the pastor and a planning committee, or the pastor and leaders of all church ministries. The critical common denominator in all of these options is the pastor. It is not an option for the pastor to be uninvolved. This is one aspect of ministry leadership that should not be delegated too far from the senior staff leader in the congregation. If the pastor does not feel secure in taking the primary leadership role, that's fine, but he or she should not be absent from this leadership opportunity; the pastor must be part of the leadership group. Select the group that makes the most sense for your setting and go for it!

Third, what is the best context for the assessment?

It's essential that whoever is involved in the assessment be given clear instructions and guidance by the facilitator/leader. Each participant in the process needs to do his or her own assessment work separate from the "group think" of committee discussion. Ratings and comments from individual assessments should be compiled, summarized, and compared before the group meets to discuss the findings. When the group convenes, the discussion of the results should focus on:

- Strengths and weaknesses discovered
- Areas of agreement and disagreement identified
- Disparity between how leaders and laity rated the church, if any
- Underlying reasons for any disagreements unearthed

- Determining together an overall summary of three strengths and three areas of concern

Fourth, how many sessions are required?
Plan on from six to ten two-hour sessions.

For the 6 sessions model:
One introductory session
One session for each of the three categories of the ten characteristics:
    Session 2 Relationship with God (characteristics 1–3)
    Session 3 Relationship within the family of God (characteristics 4–6)
    Session 4 Ministry outside the immediate family of God and management of ministry (characteristics 7–10)
Plus, two wrap-up sessions.

For the 6–10 sessions model:
Follow the 6 sessions model above, plus add a wrap-up session and 3 planning sessions. (Refer to planning section of workbook for additional ideas.)

Fifth, how long should the process take?
The shortest possible time for this process is over one or two weekends (retreat or extended meeting sessions).
The longest reasonable time is nine months.
The more likely time frame is three to four months.

Sixth, what are the models for the facilitation process from which you can choose?
There are several models possible, but let me suggest two for your consideration.

Alternative A: Short Process
  I. Introductory Session: The pastor/facilitator leads a kickoff meeting with team members designed to introduce and explain the entire dialogue and assessment process. At this meeting, an overview of the Ten Characteristics of a Healthy Church is given by one or more members of the team. Objectives and activities for this process are outlined clearly.

A. Each team member is given a workbook to use throughout the process. If workbooks are not purchased for each member, then short versions of the Leadership Team Discussion Tool need to be purchased from Vision New England. (See page 139 for ordering details or go to www.VisionNewEngland.com.)

B. The pastor distributes to members of the congregation the Congregation Assessment Tool (order in bulk from Vision New England—see page 00 for a description and information on ordering or go to www.VisionNewEngland .com) and provides a schedule for its completion.

C. Copies of individual completed assessments are compiled for the pastor/facilitator to review and analyze. If you use the assessment contained in this workbook, individual members will need to give photocopies of their responses, or their completed workbooks, to the pastor/facilitator to review. The short version of the leadership assessment tool can be compiled with the Excel spreadsheet included in the packet from Vision New England.

II. Session 2 will need to occur after the team and congregation assessments have been tabulated. In this session, the pastor/facilitator will meet with the team to discuss the findings. The pastor/facilitator presents the major findings of the healthy church assessment, focusing on:

- Ministry strengths
- Ministry shortcomings
- Areas of team assessment agreement
- Areas of team assessment disagreement
- Reasons for perceived strengths and shortcomings

III. Session 3: The pastor/facilitator leads the group in addressing the two or three key findings in greater depth. This would include:

- The key strengths of the church that can become the basis for future ministry

- The key challenges that should be improved on to avoid ministry hindrances in the future

IV. Session 4: The pastor/facilitator asks the group to dream together about what God might want the church to do in the next year or two. After brainstorming possible options, the team agrees to pray that God will continue to lead them regarding the discovery of his vision for their shared future.

V. Session 5: The pastor/facilitator guides the team in selecting the dream that the participants believe God is calling their church to pursue, and then the group (or key leader) develops a small number of action steps that will propel the church toward realizing this dream under the power of the Holy Spirit.

VI. Future sessions will include the pastor /facilitator and key leaders in the congregation who will work through the planning stages outlined later in this workbook, starting with session 6 as a brainstorming overview session for future ministry development.

Please note: An optional enhancement to this process includes soliciting input from as many members of the congregation as possible. At the same time that leadership team members are completing their church assessments, copies of the Congregation Assessment Tool (available from Vision New England, see pages 139 for details on ordering copies and compilation software or go to www.VisionNewEngland.com) could be distributed. The entire process is enhanced by the number of responses processed. Strive for the highest percentage of your congregation's participation as is achievable. In session one, when comparing team agreement and disagreement, it will be important that you also compare places where the team and the congregation were in agreement or disagreement.

Alternative B: Longer Process

I. Introductory Session: The pastor/facilitator leads a kickoff meeting with team members designed to introduce and explain the entire dialogue and assessment process. At this meeting, an overview of the Ten Characteristics of a Healthy Church is given by one or more members of the team. Objectives and activities for this process are outlined clearly.

A. Each team member is given a workbook to use throughout the process. If workbooks are not purchased for each member, then short versions of the Leadership Team Discussion Tool need to be purchased from Vision New England. (See page 139 for ordering details or go to www.VisionNewEngland.com.)

B. The pastor distributes to members of the congregation the Congregation Assessment Tool (order in bulk from Vision New England—see page 139 for a description and information on ordering or go to www.VisionNewEngland .com) and provides a schedule for its completion.

C. Copies of individual completed assessments are compiled for the pastor/facilitator to review and analyze. If you use the assessment contained in this workbook, individual members will need to give photocopies of their responses, or their completed workbooks, to the pastor/facilitator to review. The short version of the leadership assessment tool can be compiled with the Excel spreadsheet included in the packet from Vision New England.

II. Session 2 will need to occur after the team and congregation assessments have been tabulated. In this session, the pastor/facilitator will meet with the team to discuss the findings. The pastor/facilitator presents the major findings of the healthy church assessment, focusing on:
- Ministry strengths
- Ministry shortcomings
- Areas of team assessment agreement
- Areas of team assessment disagreement
- Reasons for perceived strengths and shortcomings

III. Sessions 3, 4, and 5 will focus on findings discovered in the assessment tools that focus on the three major groupings of healthy church characteristics.

Session 3 Relationship with God (characteristics 1–3)

Session 4 Relationship within family of God (characteristics 4–6)

Session 5 Ministry outside the immediate family of God and management of ministry (characteristics 7–10)

IV. Session 6 will be comprised of an overview of the above with special focus on assessing the major strengths and shortcomings of the church. This would include:
- The key strengths of the church that can become the basis for future ministry
- The key challenges that should be improved on to avoid ministry hindrances in the future

V. In session 7 the pastor/facilitator asks the group to dream together about what God may want the church to do in the next year or two. After brainstorming possible options, the team agrees to pray that God will continue to lead them regarding the discovery of his vision for their shared future.

VI. In session 8 the pastor/facilitator guides the team in selecting the dream that the participants believe God is calling their church to pursue, and then the group develops a small number of action steps that will propel the church toward realizing this dream under the power of the Holy Spirit.

VII. Future sessions will involve the pastor/facilitator and key leaders in the congregation who will work through the planning stages outlined later in this workbook.

Seventh, when can you get started?

Now! Before conducting session 2 of the assessment process, please read the next chapter on conflict resolution, because conflict will inevitably be part of the process.

Guidelines for Leaders on Conflict Resolution

One promise I can make to every team engaged in the process of assessing the health of your church: Conflict is inevitable! As your team continues to dig into significant issues regarding the past and current status of your ministry effectiveness, it's certain that members will approach topics from a variety of vantage points. The dialogue and assessment process is designed to be very relational, encouraging full involvement by every participant. The questions for you to wrestle with are: What are the value-added benefits of conflict and how is it to be redeemed and resolved when it occurs?

I am one of those crazy people who sees the positive side of conflict in congregations—if it is properly handled. The problem is most of us in local churches handle conflict poorly and therefore consider conflict a threat to relational health and ministry effectiveness. Frankly, I have been a part of enough conflict in my ministry career to see both sides of the same conflict "coin." The underside of the coin is dark and often painful. It's on this side of the coin that we say things that hurt another's feelings, misuse trust by shunning the needs of a loved one, express inappropriate body language that speaks louder than our words, and/or discredit another believer by gossiping about him or her. These are just a few of the reasons why conflicts emerge. Most of our conflicts share one or more common root causes:

Communication breakdown. Either we don't communicate enough or we communicate inappropriately. It's rare to find relationships where there is too much communication!

Expectations that are too high. We get disappointed when our unexpressed or overly high expectations are not met. One of my mentors once told me, "Expectations equal disappointments, so be careful how lofty you allow your expectations to get!"

Lack of relationship building. We don't take the appropriate amount of time to really get to know the other person(s) we are working with, and as a result we make assumptions of others that oftentimes are totally inaccurate.

Speaking to the wrong person. We tend to vent our frustrations about others to those who will give us a listening ear, all the while sidestepping the biblical approach of dealing directly with our brothers and sisters in Christ who have offended us.

Inappropriate responses to conflict. We all have a "preferred reaction" to conflict when it arises, most often learned from childhood as we observed the adults around us deal with conflict themselves. We end up choosing either to bully or manipulate our way to victory or we back down to a more powerful and aggressive personality, seeking peace at any price, or we back out and avoid the relationship altogether, or we compromise so that as many as possible are satisfied at least to a minimum level of contentment. Few of us choose the route of resolution of the conflict so that all parties are fully engaged in working through whatever issues land on the table and need to be settled.

Spiritual immaturity. We see the true depth of individuals when conflicts erupt. Often the most strident ones in the process are the most immature. Those who can calmly, rationally, and empathetically seek resolution are the ones who are in essence expressing their depth of maturity, wisdom, and insight.

It's not the fact that conflict occurs in the congregation that is of primary importance, but how we handle it when it arises. Those charged with leadership responsibilities in the local church are to take their God-given calling seriously and work to effectively resolve every conflict that erupts along the way. It's not healthy to sweep conflicts under the carpet. Far too many churches have done exactly that and their buildings are filled with bumpy carpets as a result. Bumpy carpets are not easy to walk on, they put you off balance, and they make you trip along the way. Leaders need to be willing to lift the carpets at all edges and sweep out the conflict "dust balls" that have developed over time and have been left unattended. The goal is not a conflict-free congregation; the goal is a congregation that knows how to directly, discreetly, and in a Christ-honoring fashion resolve conflict so that each carpet is safe to walk on!

Conflict is a biblical reality. In the Scriptures we read of dozens of cases of conflict (Genesis 4—Cain and Abel; Genesis 37—Joseph and his brothers; 1 Samuel 18–19—Saul and David; Matthew 20:24—Jesus' disciples; Luke 10:38–42 —Martha and Mary; John 2:12–17—Jesus and the money changers; Acts 6:1–6—overlooked widows—just to name a few!). Therefore, when the people of God find themselves in conflicting situations today, it should not come as a surprise to us! Conflict was an inevitable reality for the biblical characters and remains a part of our relationships as well.

Conflict not only comes in all shapes and sizes, it also emerges in layers of intensity. On the lowest level, conflicts emerge because of low morale or a lack of passionate purpose. It's here that we see evidences of a lack of overall enthusiasm about church life and service. It's a ho-hum existence that leads to the more petty conflicts surrounding issues of minor importance. Over a period of time, however, the intensity of the conflicts grows, usually because of excessive gossiping about one another. For example, what began as minor complaints about the color of the carpet and drapes develops into maligning the personalities of those who chose the carpet and drapes. This type of conflict can degenerate further into open disputes, with factions warring for control of the church. It can even lead to sabotage, which either undermines the leadership or leads to church splits. The progression from one level to the next leads to an eruption that's totally inappropriate and unhealthy for the people of God.

The fruit of unresolved conflict in congregations is not a pretty sight. There is not only little spiritual growth in such settings but also a downward spiral that affects giving, attendance, and programmatic effectiveness, which can be devastating for a church. The poor reputation of the congregation in the community leads to ineffectiveness at every level. Unfortunately, internal power struggles can sometimes take a whole generation to overcome. All of the results of unresolved conflicts lead to an embarrassing smear on the kingdom of God and the church of Jesus Christ.

My colleague Bob Ludwig, when teaching pastors and church leaders on this subject, offers ten practical principles that lead to healthy conflict resolution:

1. *Be proactive.* Most leaders hope that conflict will just go away on its own. Don't be fooled; it rarely does. Leadership means being proactive in all aspects of ministry service, including the ability to direct others into a healthy resolution of conflict. In speaking of spiritual gifts, the apostle Paul reminds us, "If it is leadership, let him govern diligently" (Rom. 12:8).

2. *Listen carefully.* People frequently will feel that "they haven't been heard." James 1:19 urges us to be "quick to listen, slow to speak, and slow to become angry." The posture of a genuine listening ear produces health in relationships and leads to empathetic understanding of others. When Jesus was with the woman at the well, he listened carefully to her reaction to his full awareness of her story (John 4), and eternal life was offered to quench her thirst.

3. *Separate the problem.* Any kind of significant conflict usually has several complex roots. It's important, therefore, to take one issue at a time. As you begin to peel away the layers of the problem, you are better prepared to confront the real issues involved. When Jesus dealt with Martha (Luke 10:38–42), he separated the distraction of her preparations from the one thing that mattered most—her heart inclined fully in his direction.

4. *Get the facts.* There is no substitute for getting everyone to agree to the facts. This is oftentimes the best place to begin when resolving conflicts within your congregation. Force those involved to give the facts before expressing feelings or predetermined conclusions. The Jerusalem Council (Acts 15:6–11) rehearsed theology, but they also cited the facts!

5. *Defuse the emotion.* People involved in conflicts must express their feelings, and the feelings expressed must be acknowledged and legitimized. The expression of those feelings should be done in a God-honoring way, remembering that our words are only 10 percent of our total message. Our tone of voice and body language constitute the majority of our message and should be kept in check when expressing our feelings. In Acts 6 the apostles were wise in tending to the needs of the widows through others that were filled with the Holy Spirit, instead of acting on emotional impulse and ultimately neglecting their own mission of prayer and the ministry of the Word of God.

6. *Be fair.* When charged with the responsibility of resolving a conflict, it is vitally important that the leader show no favoritism. If there is assumed bias in the situation, then find ways of balancing that with creativity and sensitivity to all parties involved. In the Acts 6 account, when the apostles were made aware of the Greek *and* Hebrew widows who were overlooked, they responded fairly to both groups.

7. *Provide breathing room.* If a conflict has developed over several years, it won't be solved in a weekend! The common de facto theology that we espouse is that conversion is instantaneous; sanctification is quick. The correct theological understanding in conversion is instantaneous; sanctification is a long, slow, gradual process! For we "are being transformed into his likeness with ever-increasing glory, which comes from the Lord" (2 Cor. 3:18). Give the time necessary for healing and restoration of relationships. It won't happen overnight.

8. *Give perspective.* Tactfully play the role of the other side on occasion. Put the Golden Rule into action and "do to others as you would have them do to you" (Luke 6:31), by loving them enough to be completely honest with them. It's hard to get the right balance when you've listened to and challenged the involved parties, but finding that objective perspective is always the goal.

9. *Communicate clearly.* Effective communication is hard work. Many leaders try to be diplomatic and end up being very undiplomatic. As Jesus once said, "Simply let your 'Yes' be 'Yes,' and your 'No,' 'No,'" (Matt. 5:37). Clarity of thought and instruction will lead to focused decisions about how to clear up the conflicts you confront.

10. *Accept diversity.* You won't always get unanimous agreement from each party involved in a conflict. It's better to know that from the beginning and develop ways to work with divergence of opinion all along the way. We are members of the same body, but with different functions and purposes—one body made up of many parts (1 Cor. 12:12).

Resolving Conflict Is a Matter of the Heart

When all is said and done, conflict is only resolvable when our hearts are open to the Spirit of God directing us to attitudes of unconditional love and grace. As a team, you may need to open the Scriptures and ask God to reveal his heart to you as you work through tense moments in ministry together. Places to turn include: Rom. 12:9–18; 1 Cor. 13:4–8; Eph. 4:22–32; Col. 3:12–17; Heb. 12:1–3; and James 3:13–18.

Speaking the truth in love is the only way to develop maturity in relationships. As a team, commit together to love truth and truthfully love and you'll go a long way together—even when the going gets rough! As you make such a commitment, you will need to focus a lot of your time and energy on team building around the joyful discipline of prayer. It is only by the power of the Spirit of God in your midst that you will be able to function with a forgiving heart toward one another. We can't do this in our own strength!

As you pray in times of conflict:

- Ask God to show you if there is a log in your eye before talking to the other person about a splinter in his or her eye
- Ask God to help you defuse your anger so that you can talk openly, honestly, and lovingly with the other person
- Ask God to show you your own preconceived ideas and biases and invite him to reshape them according to his will
- Ask God to bless and multiply the ministry of his Spirit through the person with whom you are in conflict
- Ask God to bring healing, hope, and renewal to your church as a result of working through these issues in a way that honors Christ and one another.

Out of these times of Scripture study and prayer, be sure that when confronting a brother or sister in Christ, you do so in a manner befitting a child of God. Go to the person directly and approach your resolution efforts with humility and love, recognizing that when you point a finger at another, there are three pointing back at you! Ask questions whenever possible to get all the facts and feelings straightened out and fully understood. Be quick to listen, slow to speak, and slow to anger. Speak the truth in love! Be sure to display mercy and grace instead of criticism and judgment. Do your best to show the other person that you care very deeply about him or her as a person and that you desire the very best relationship possible. Ask for forgiveness and freely grant forgiveness. Encourage the other person and represent the love of Christ in every way you communicate. God will bless this kind

of heartfelt effort—for his glory and for the building up of his church (never mind the spiritual renewal *you* will experience!).

One Other Idea

If your team is interested in spending one of your dialogue sessions focusing on a discussion around the subject of conflict resolution, here are some discussion questions to consider:

1. How do you handle conflict? Do you try to win, withdraw, yield, or compromise? Is it a fight to the finish? What are the acceptable and unacceptable styles of handling conflict in our church and on our team?
2. Conflict left unattended can produce a deadly cancer in relationships. What will it take for us to always choose to resolve our conflicts rather than let them fester and, if left unattended, grow?
3. Read together Ephesians 4:22–32 and discuss the ways in which unhealthy anger hinders the process of conflict resolution. How can anger be avoided and/or dealt with in our ministry setting?
4. Genuine relationships give permission to "speak the truth in love" to one another. Truthful confrontation balanced with loving affirmation produces the best results. Into whose emotional bank account do you need to deposit a word of loving affirmation this coming week?
5. Pray for one another and for your team that God would help you resolve every conflict that comes your way throughout this dialogue, assessment, and planning process, and that the entire church will learn how to effectively deal with conflicts as they inevitably arise in the context of your ministry.

Before you begin the exciting journey before you, let's pray . . .

Almighty and most merciful Father, grant, we pray, an attitude of expectancy about the process on which we are about to embark. Help us see our church in as realistic a light as possible, without becoming crit-

ical toward others either past or present, who have shaped our life together here in our local church. We know that you love your bride, the church of Jesus Christ. In love let us be found faithful in our dialogue and in our assessment of the health of our ministry setting, so that we may grow together in our understanding of your will for us. We trust you to guide us throughout this process as you work through our leaders in addressing very real issues about our congregation and our shared ministry in this community and around the world. We open up ourselves to your tender hand of guiding grace. Lead us forward in hope and love. We pray in our matchless Savior's name, Jesus Christ. Amen.

Part 2
Time for Dialogue and Assessment

The following pages will take you through a series of evaluative exercises that will assist you and your team in assessing the health and vitality of your local church. Ask each member of your team to complete these exercises in anticipation of a Spirit-led process of dialogue and evaluation. Each of the characteristics of a healthy church need to be explored in order to achieve a well-rounded understanding of the current health status of your local church ministry. This essential step will assist you in formulating plans for the future that maximize your strengths while enhancing areas needing additional attention and strengthening. Pray that God will enlighten you throughout this process of discerning his will for your congregation.

Ten Characteristics of a Healthy Church

A healthy church is prayerful in all of the following aspects of church life and ministry, is reliant on God's power and the authority of his Word, and values:

1. God's Empowering Presence
2. God-Exalting Worship
3. Spiritual Disciplines
4. Learning and Growing in Community
5. A Commitment to Loving and Caring Relationships
6. Servant-Leadership Development
7. An Outward Focus
8. Wise Administration and Accountability
9. Networking with the Body of Christ
10. Stewardship and Generosity

God's Empowering Presence

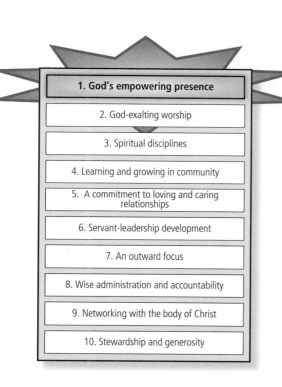

1. God's empowering presence
2. God-exalting worship
3. Spiritual disciplines
4. Learning and growing in community
5. A commitment to loving and caring relationships
6. Servant-leadership development
7. An outward focus
8. Wise administration and accountability
9. Networking with the body of Christ
10. Stewardship and generosity

The healthy church actively seeks the Holy Spirit's direction and empowerment for its daily life and ministry.

In seeking to understand and implement God's will, the church:

- articulates a clear understanding of who God is
- teaches the "whole counsel of God" and relates it to the contemporary Christian church
- emphasizes a supernatural-reliance instead of a self-reliance
- creates enthusiasm about being a part of the kingdom of God
- prays for God's initiative and anticipates that God will act
- encourages its leaders to be change agents under God's guidance
- desires the fruit of the Spirit for all its members
- seeks the gifts of the Spirit within the body

The Spirit himself testifies with our spirit that we are God's children.

Romans 8:16

The following Scriptures from Jesus' life and teaching relate to God's empowering presence. Reflect on them before evaluating your church on this characteristic.

Matthew 18:20 *For where two or three come together in my name, there am I with them.*

Luke 11:11–13 *If you then, though you are evil, know how to give good gifts to your children, how much more will your Father in heaven give the Holy Spirit to those who ask him!* (v. 13).

Luke 11:14–26 *But if I drive out demons by the finger of God, then the kingdom of God has come to you* (v. 20).

Luke 17:20–21 *The kingdom of God does not come with your careful observation . . . because the kingdom of God is within you.*

Luke 24:49 *I am going to send you what my Father has promised; but stay in the city until you have been clothed with power from on high.*

John 14:16–17 *And I will ask the Father, and he will give you another Counselor to be with you forever—the Spirit of truth. . . . you know him, for he lives with you and will be in you.*

John 14:26 *But the Counselor, the Holy Spirit . . . will teach you all things.*

John 15:5 *If a man remains in me and I in him, he will bear much fruit; apart from me you can do nothing.*

John 17:22–23 *I have given them the glory that you gave me, that they may be one as we are one: I in them and you in me.*

Parable of the Good Shepherd: John 10:1–18 *When he has brought out all his own, he goes on ahead of them, and his sheep follow him because they know his voice* (v. 4). *I have come that they may have life, and have it to the full* (v. 10).

Assess your church in regard to its health in the following areas:

Our church:

Articulates
a clear understanding of who God is.

How effective are we at living out this element of ministry in our church?

Not Effective   Very Effective

1   2   3   4   5   6   7   8   9   10

Personal notes (optional):

Creates
enthusiasm about being a part of the kingdom of God.

How effective are we at living out this element of ministry in our church?

Not Effective   Very Effective

1   2   3   4   5   6   7   8   9   10

Personal notes (optional):

Teaches
the "whole counsel of God" and relates it to the contemporary Christian church.

How effective are we at living out this element of ministry in our church?

Not Effective   Very Effective

1   2   3   4   5   6   7   8   9   10

Personal notes (optional):

Prays
for God's initiative and anticipates that God will act.

How effective are we at living out this element of ministry in our church?

Not Effective   Very Effective

1   2   3   4   5   6   7   8   9   10

Personal notes (optional):

Emphasizes
a supernatural-reliance instead of a self-reliance.

How effective are we at living out this element of ministry in our church?

Not Effective   Very Effective

1   2   3   4   5   6   7   8   9   10

Personal notes (optional):

Encourages
its leaders to be change agents under God's guidance.

How effective are we at living out this element of ministry in our church?

Not Effective   Very Effective

1   2   3   4   5   6   7   8   9   10

Personal notes (optional):

Desires
the fruit of the Spirit for all its members.

How effective are we at living out this element of ministry in our church?

Not Effective   Very Effective

1   2   3   4   5   6   7   8   9   10

Personal notes (optional):

Seeks
the gifts of the Spirit within the body.

How effective are we at living out this element of ministry in our church?

Not Effective   Very Effective

1   2   3   4   5   6   7   8   9   10

Personal notes (optional):

Overall Rating
How effective are we at living out this characteristic in our church (average score)?

Not Effective   Very Effective

1   2   3   4   5   6   7   8   9   10

Personal notes (optional):

God's Empowering Presence

1. *What* are we doing to live out this characteristic today? At present what are our strengths? What are we doing well?

2. *Where* do we want to be in the characteristic "God's Empowering Presence" in the next year or two? What is our *dream* for the future?

3. *How* will we get where we want to be in living out "God's Empowering Presence" in the next year or two?

God-Exalting Worship

The healthy church gathers regularly as the local expression of the body of Christ to worship God in ways that engage the heart, mind, soul, and strength of the people.

1. God's empowering presence
2. God-exalting worship
3. Spiritual disciplines
4. Learning and growing in community
5. A commitment to loving and caring relationships
6. Servant-leadership development
7. An outward focus
8. Wise administration and accountability
9. Networking with the body of Christ
10. Stewardship and generosity

Corporate worship is the ongoing reminder of:

- the lordship of Christ
- the power of the Holy Spirit
- the redemptive work of God the Father among us
- the truths of God's Word
- our need to share the gospel
- our mandate to serve others in need

Worship includes such elements as:

- prayer—adoration, praise, thanksgiving, confession, and petition
- reading of Scripture
- preaching from God's Word for instruction, guidance, encouragement, comfort, challenge, and rebuke
- baptism and communion
- singing songs and hymns that praise God and encourage us as believers
- affirmation of those truths we believe
- giving our tithes and offerings
- dedication to the service of God in our lives

Yet a time is coming and has now come when the true worshipers will worship the Father in spirit and truth, for they are the kind of worshipers the Father seeks.

John 4:23

The following Scriptures from Jesus' life and teaching relate to God-exalting worship. Reflect on them before evaluating your church on this characteristic.

Matthew 4:10 *Worship the Lord your God, and serve him only.*

Matthew 15:8–9 *Their hearts are far from me. They worship me in vain.*

Mark 11:9–10 *Those who went ahead and those who followed shouted, "Hosanna!" "Blessed is he who comes in the name of the Lord!" . . . "Hosanna in the highest!"*

Luke 1:46–55 *My soul glorifies the Lord and my spirit rejoices in God my Savior (vv. 46–47).*

Luke 1:67–79 *Praise be to the Lord, the God of Israel, because he has come and has redeemed his people. . . . to show mercy to our fathers and to remember his holy covenant (vv. 68, 72).*

Luke 7:36–50 *She began to wet his feet with her tears. Then she wiped them with her hair, kissed them and poured perfume on them (v. 38).*

Luke 17:15–16 *One of them, when he saw he was healed, came back, praising God in a loud voice. He threw himself at Jesus' feet and thanked him.*

Luke 18:35–43 *Immediately he received his sight and followed Jesus, praising God. When all the people saw it, they also praised God (v. 43).*

Luke 19:37–40 *The whole crowd of disciples began joyfully to praise God in loud voices for all the miracles they had seen (v. 37). "I tell you," he replied, "if they keep quiet, the stones will cry out" (v. 40).*

Luke 24:52–53 *Then they worshiped him and returned to Jerusalem with great joy. And they stayed continually at the temple, praising God.*

John 4:21–24 *Yet a time is coming and has now come when the true worshipers will worship the Father in spirit and truth, for they are the kind of worshipers the Father seeks (v. 23).*

Parables of the Lost Sheep, the Lost Coin, and the Lost Son: Luke 15:3–32 *God-exalting worship takes place in heaven (and also on earth) every time a sinner genuinely repents, as evidenced in these three parables.*

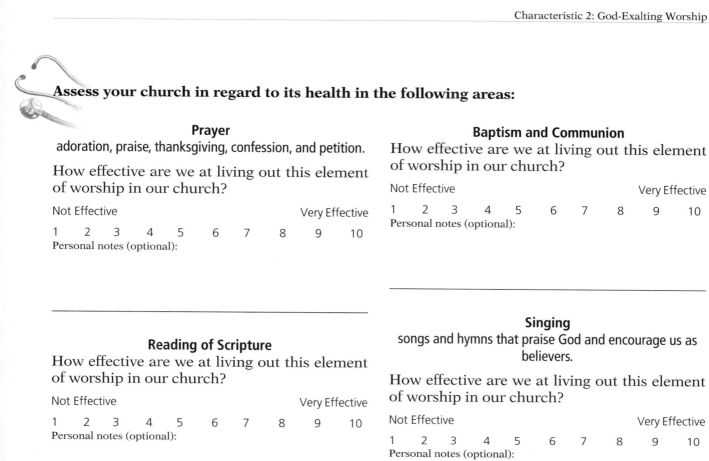

Assess your church in regard to its health in the following areas:

Prayer
adoration, praise, thanksgiving, confession, and petition.

How effective are we at living out this element of worship in our church?

Not Effective   Very Effective

1   2   3   4   5   6   7   8   9   10

Personal notes (optional):

Baptism and Communion
How effective are we at living out this element of worship in our church?

Not Effective   Very Effective

1   2   3   4   5   6   7   8   9   10

Personal notes (optional):

Reading of Scripture
How effective are we at living out this element of worship in our church?

Not Effective   Very Effective

1   2   3   4   5   6   7   8   9   10

Personal notes (optional):

Singing
songs and hymns that praise God and encourage us as believers.

How effective are we at living out this element of worship in our church?

Not Effective   Very Effective

1   2   3   4   5   6   7   8   9   10

Personal notes (optional):

Preaching
from God's Word for instruction, guidance, encouragement, comfort, challenge, and rebuke.

How effective are we at living out this element of worship in our church?

Not Effective   Very Effective

1   2   3   4   5   6   7   8   9   10

Personal notes (optional):

Giving
of our tithes and offerings.

How effective are we at living out this element of worship in our church?

Not Effective   Very Effective

1   2   3   4   5   6   7   8   9   10

Personal notes (optional):

Affirmation
of those truths we believe.

How effective are we at living out this element of worship in our church?

Not Effective   Very Effective

1   2   3   4   5   6   7   8   9   10

Personal notes (optional):

God-Exalting Worship

1. *What* are we doing to live out this characteristic today? At present what are our strengths? What are we doing well?

Dedication
to the service of God in our lives.

How effective are we at living out this element of worship in our church?

Not Effective   Very Effective

1   2   3   4   5   6   7   8   9   10

Personal notes (optional):

2. *Where* do we want to be in the characteristic "God-Exalting Worship" in the next year or two? What is our *dream* for the future?

Overall Rating

How effective are we at living out this characteristic in our church (average score)?

Not Effective   Very Effective

1   2   3   4   5   6   7   8   9   10

Personal notes (optional):

3. *How* will we get where we want to be in living out "God-Exalting Worship" in the next year or two?

Spiritual Disciplines

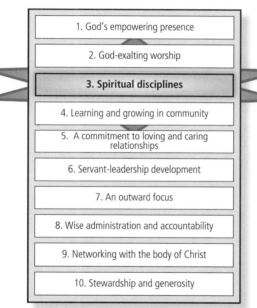

1. God's empowering presence

2. God-exalting worship

3. Spiritual disciplines

4. Learning and growing in community

5. A commitment to loving and caring relationships

6. Servant-leadership development

7. An outward focus

8. Wise administration and accountability

9. Networking with the body of Christ

10. Stewardship and generosity

The healthy church provides training, models, and resources for members of all ages to develop their daily spiritual disciplines.

These disciplines include such things as:

- Bible study
- personal worship
- confession
- petition for ourselves and others
- journaling
- recognizing and utilizing our spiritual gifts
- listening to God's voice
- pursuing God's will
- growing to Christ-like maturity
- developing a strong sense of integrity
- growing as a person in body, mind, and spirit

But the wisdom that comes from heaven is first of all pure; then peace-loving, considerate, submissive, full of mercy and good fruit, impartial and sincere.

James 3:17

The following Scriptures from Jesus' life and teaching relate to spiritual disciplines. Reflect on them before evaluating your church on this characteristic.

Matthew 4:4 *Jesus answered, "It is written: 'Man does not live on bread alone, but on every word that comes from the mouth of God.'"*

Matthew 6:5–14 *Do not be like the hypocrites. . . . Go into your room, close the door and pray to your Father. . . . This, then, is how you should pray: "Our Father in heaven, hallowed be your name . . ." (vv. 5–6, 9).*

Matthew 6:16–18 *Do not look somber as the hypocrites do. . . . put oil on your head and wash your face (vv. 16–17).*

Matthew 6:33 *But seek first his kingdom and his righteousness, and all these things will be given to you as well.*

Mark 1:35 *Very early . . . while it was still dark, Jesus . . . went off to a solitary place, where he prayed.*

Luke 14:26 *If anyone comes to me and does not hate his father and mother, his wife and children, his brothers and sisters—yes, even his own life—he cannot be my disciple.*

Luke 14:28–33 *In the same way, any of you who does not give up everything he has cannot be my disciple (v. 33).*

Luke 18:1–8 *Jesus told his disciples a parable to show them that they should always pray and not give up (v. 1).*

John 12:26 *Whoever serves me must follow me; and where I am, my servant also will be. My Father will honor the one who serves me.*

John 13:34–35 *A new command I give you: Love one another. As I have loved you, so you must love one another (v. 34).*

John 15:7–8 *If you remain in me and my words remain in you, ask whatever you wish, and it will be given you. This is to my Father's glory, that you bear much fruit, showing yourselves to be my disciples.*

The Parable of the Wise and Foolish Builders: Luke 6:46–49 *Why do you call me, "Lord, Lord," and do not do what I say? I will show you what he is like who comes to me and hears my words and puts them into practice. He is like a man building a house, who dug down deep and laid the foundation on rock. When a flood came, the torrent struck that house but could not shake it, because it was well built (vv. 46–48).*

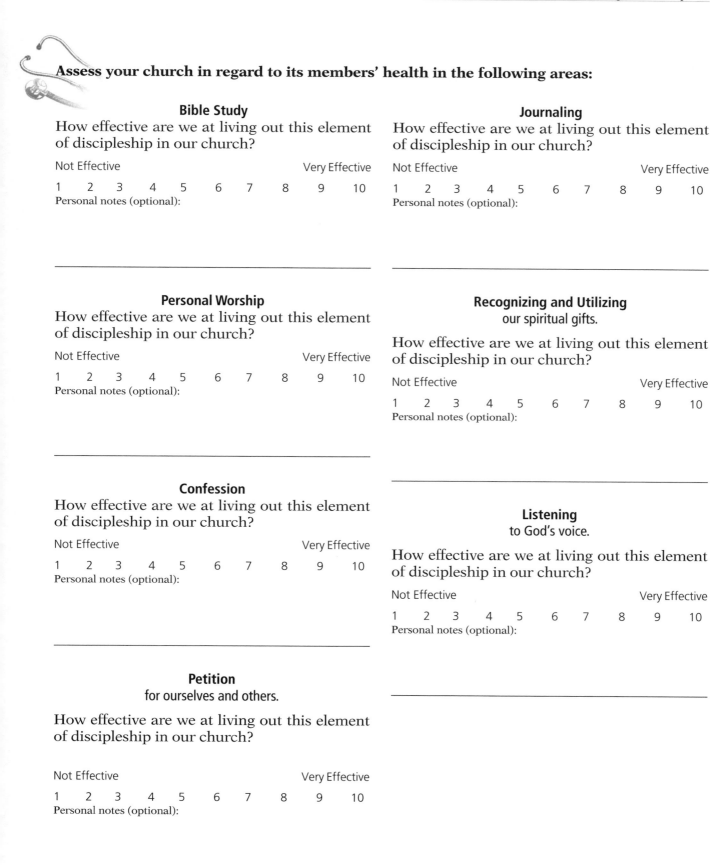

Assess your church in regard to its members' health in the following areas:

Bible Study

How effective are we at living out this element of discipleship in our church?

Not Effective   Very Effective

1   2   3   4   5   6   7   8   9   10

Personal notes (optional):

Journaling

How effective are we at living out this element of discipleship in our church?

Not Effective   Very Effective

1   2   3   4   5   6   7   8   9   10

Personal notes (optional):

Personal Worship

How effective are we at living out this element of discipleship in our church?

Not Effective   Very Effective

1   2   3   4   5   6   7   8   9   10

Personal notes (optional):

Recognizing and Utilizing
our spiritual gifts.

How effective are we at living out this element of discipleship in our church?

Not Effective   Very Effective

1   2   3   4   5   6   7   8   9   10

Personal notes (optional):

Confession

How effective are we at living out this element of discipleship in our church?

Not Effective   Very Effective

1   2   3   4   5   6   7   8   9   10

Personal notes (optional):

Listening
to God's voice.

How effective are we at living out this element of discipleship in our church?

Not Effective   Very Effective

1   2   3   4   5   6   7   8   9   10

Personal notes (optional):

Petition
for ourselves and others.

How effective are we at living out this element of discipleship in our church?

Not Effective   Very Effective

1   2   3   4   5   6   7   8   9   10

Personal notes (optional):

Pursuing
God's will.

How effective are we at living out this element of discipleship in our church?

Not Effective   Very Effective

1   2   3   4   5   6   7   8   9   10

Personal notes (optional):

Growing
to Christ-like maturity.

How effective are we at living out this element of discipleship in our church?

Not Effective   Very Effective

1   2   3   4   5   6   7   8   9   10

Personal notes (optional):

Developing
a strong sense of integrity.

How effective are we at living out this element of discipleship in our church?

Not Effective   Very Effective

1   2   3   4   5   6   7   8   9   10

Personal notes (optional):

Growing
as a person in body, mind, and spirit.

How effective are we at living out this element of discipleship in our church?

Not Effective   Very Effective

1   2   3   4   5   6   7   8   9   10

Personal notes (optional):

Overall Rating

How effective are we at living out this characteristic in our church (average score)?

Not Effective   Very Effective

1   2   3   4   5   6   7   8   9   10

Personal notes (optional):

Spiritual Disciplines

1. *What* are we doing to live out this characteristic today? At present what are our strengths? What are we doing well?

2. *Where* do we want to be in the characteristic "Spiritual Disciplines" in the next year or two? What is our *dream* for the future?

3. *How* will we get where we want to be in living out "Spiritual Disciplines" in the next year or two?

Learning and Growing in Community

The healthy church encourages believers to grow in their walk with God and with one another in the context of a safe, affirming environment.

The healthy church accomplishes this objective by:

- enabling people to see Jesus clearly
- helping people know his will for them
- equipping people to follow him in all of life
- helping each person, either clergy or layperson, to find his or her calling either at home or abroad
- encouraging people to discover and use their God-given gifts and training them accordingly
- providing settings for members to come together for teaching, prayer, sharing, and service

It does these things through:

- individual mentors
- small-group Bible studies and discipleship groups
- a variety of training and learning opportunities

1. God's empowering presence
2. God-exalting worship
3. Spiritual disciplines
4. Learning and growing in community
5. A commitment to loving and caring relationships
6. Servant-leadership development
7. An outward focus
8. Wise administration and accountability
9. Networking with the body of Christ
10. Stewardship and generosity

> Let us therefore make every effort to do what leads to peace and to mutual edification.
>
> Romans 14:19

The following Scriptures from Jesus' life and teaching relate to learning and growing in community. Reflect on them before evaluating your church on this characteristic.

Matthew 5–7 *Now when he saw the crowds, he went up on a mountainside and sat down. His disciples came to him, and he began to teach them (5:1). The crowds were amazed at his teaching, because he taught as one who had authority, and not as their teachers of the law (7:28–29).*

Matthew 7:12 *So in everything, do to others what you would have them do to you, for this sums up the Law and the Prophets.*

Matthew 14:15–21 *"Bring them here to me," he said. And he directed the people to sit down on the grass. Taking the five loaves and the two fish and looking up to heaven, he gave thanks and broke the loaves. . . . They all ate and were satisfied (vv. 18–20).*

Luke 8:19–21 *He replied, "My mother and brothers are those who hear God's word and put it into practice" (v. 21).*

Luke 18:43 *Immediately he received his sight and followed Jesus, praising God. When all the people saw it, they also praised God.*

Parable of the Sower: Matthew 13:1–9, 18–23 *When anyone hears the message about the kingdom and does not understand it, the evil one comes and snatches away what was sown in his heart. This is the seed sown along the path. The one who received the seed that fell on rocky places is the man who hears the word and at once receives it with joy. . . . When trouble or persecution comes because of the word, he quickly falls away. The one who received the seed that fell among the thorns is the man who hears the word, but the worries of this life and the deceitfulness of wealth choke it, making it unfruitful. But the one who received the seed that fell on good soil is the man who hears the word and understands it. He produces a crop, yielding a hundred, sixty or thirty times what was sown (vv. 19–23).*

Parable of the Householder: Matthew 13:52 *He said to them, "Therefore every teacher of the law who has been instructed about the kingdom of heaven is like the owner of a house who brings out of his storeroom new treasures as well as old."*

Assess your church in regard to its health in the following areas:

Enabling
people to see Jesus clearly.

How effective are we at living out this element of ministry in our church?

Not Effective   Very Effective

1   2   3   4   5   6   7   8   9   10

Personal notes (optional):

_____

Helping
each person, either clergy or layperson, to find his or her calling either at home or abroad.

How effective are we at living out this element of ministry in our church?

Not Effective   Very Effective

1   2   3   4   5   6   7   8   9   10

Personal notes (optional):

_____

Helping
people know his will for them.

How effective are we at living out this element of ministry in our church?

Not Effective   Very Effective

1   2   3   4   5   6   7   8   9   10

Personal notes (optional):

_____

Encouraging
people to discover and use their God-given gifts and training them accordingly.

How effective are we at living out this element of ministry in our church?

Not Effective   Very Effective

1   2   3   4   5   6   7   8   9   10

Personal notes (optional):

_____

Equipping
people to follow him in all of life.

How effective are we at living out this element of ministry in our church?

Not Effective   Very Effective

1   2   3   4   5   6   7   8   9   10

Personal notes (optional):

_____

Providing
settings for members to come together for teaching, prayer, sharing, and service.

How effective are we at living out this element of ministry in our church?

Not Effective   Very Effective

1   2   3   4   5   6   7   8   9   10

Personal notes (optional):

_____

Individual Mentors

How effective are we at living out this element of ministry in our church?

Not Effective   Very Effective

1   2   3   4   5   6   7   8   9   10

Personal notes (optional):

Small-Group
Bible studies and discipleship groups.

How effective are we at living out this element of ministry in our church?

Not Effective   Very Effective

1   2   3   4   5   6   7   8   9   10

Personal notes (optional):

A Variety of Training and Learning Opportunities

How effective are we at living out this element of ministry in our church?

Not Effective   Very Effective

1   2   3   4   5   6   7   8   9   10

Personal notes (optional):

Overall Rating

How effective are we at living out this characteristic in our church (average score)?

Not Effective   Very Effective

1   2   3   4   5   6   7   8   9   10

Personal notes (optional):

Learning and Growing in Community

1. *What* are we doing to live out this characteristic today? At present what are our strengths? What are we doing well?

2. *Where* do we want to be in the characteristic "Learning and Growing in Community" in the next year or two? What is our *dream* for the future?

3. *How* will we get where we want to be in living out "Learning and Growing in Community" in the next year or two?

A Commitment to Loving and Caring Relationships

The healthy church is intentional in its efforts to build loving, caring relationships within families, between members, and within the community we serve.

1. God's empowering presence
2. God-exalting worship
3. Spiritual disciplines
4. Learning and growing in community
5. A commitment to loving and caring relationships
6. Servant-leadership development
7. An outward focus
8. Wise administration and accountability
9. Networking with the body of Christ
10. Stewardship and generosity

The healthy church understands, models, teaches, and affirms the essential elements of quality relationships and recognizes the needs of those who come from dysfunctional families.

The body serves as an affirming place for marriage and family life, including single adults, senior adults, and all phases of family development.

The healthy church builds relationships within the body of Christ through:

- modeling authenticity and affirming it in others
- sharing our lives with one another
- caring for one another
- open communication
- conflict resolution
- forgiveness
- healing
- bearing one another's burdens

The healthy church acknowledges and encourages great diversity within the body of Christ and teaches its members how to work together, disagree with love and respect, and creatively resolve conflicts. It includes people of different ages, races, ethnic groups, socioeconomic groups, previous church affiliations (or no affiliation), and stages of spiritual maturity.

> This is how we know what love is: Jesus Christ laid down his life for us. And we ought to lay down our lives for our brothers.
>
> 1 John 3:16

The following Scriptures from Jesus' life and teaching relate to a commitment to loving and caring relationships. Reflect on them before evaluating your church on this characteristic.

Matthew 5:43–48 *Love your enemies and pray for those who persecute you, that you may be sons of your Father in heaven* (vv. 44–45).

Matthew 18:15–20 *If your brother sins against you, go and show him his fault, just between the two of you. . . . But if he will not listen, take one or two others along. . . . If he refuses to listen to them, tell it to the church* (vv. 15–17).

Matthew 22:37–39 *Jesus replied, "'Love the Lord your God with all your heart and with all your soul and with all your mind.' This is the first and greatest commandment. And the second is like it, 'Love your neighbor as yourself.'"*

Mark 2:1–12 *Some men came, bringing to him a paralytic, carried by four of them. Since they could not get him to Jesus because of the crowd, they made an opening in the roof above Jesus and, after digging through it, lowered the mat the paralyzed man was lying on. When Jesus saw their faith . . .* (vv. 3–5).

Mark 11:25 *And when you stand praying, if you hold anything against anyone, forgive him.*

John 15:12 *My command is this: Love each other as I have loved you.*

John 21:15–17 *Jesus said, "Feed my sheep"* (v. 15).

Parable of the Unmerciful Servant: Matthew 18:21–35 *Then Peter came to Jesus and asked, "Lord, how many times shall I forgive my brother when he sins against me? Up to seven times?"*

Jesus answered, "I tell you, not seven times, but seventy-seven times" (vv. 21–22).

Then the master called the servant in. "You wicked servant," he said, "I canceled all that debt of yours because you begged me to. Shouldn't you have had mercy on your fellow servant just as I had on you?" In anger his master turned him over to the jailers to be tortured, until he should pay back all he owed.

This is how my heavenly Father will treat each of you unless you forgive your brother from your heart (vv. 32–35).

Parable of the Good Samaritan: Luke 10:30–37 *"Which of these three do you think was a neighbor to the man who fell into the hands of robbers?"*

The expert in the law replied, "The one who had mercy on him."

Jesus told him, "Go and do likewise" (vv. 36–37).

Assess your church in regard to its health in the following areas:

Understanding, Modeling, Teaching, and Affirming
the essential elements of quality relationships and recognizing the needs of those who come from dysfunctional families.

How effective are we at living out this element of ministry in our church?

Not Effective   Very Effective

1   2   3   4   5   6   7   8   9   10

Personal notes (optional):

Serving
as an affirming place for marriage and family life, including single adults, senior adults, and all phases of family development.

How effective are we at living out this element of ministry in our church?

Not Effective   Very Effective

1   2   3   4   5   6   7   8   9   10

Personal notes (optional):

Building Relationships within the Body of Christ
through modeling authenticity and affirming it in others.

How effective are we at living out this element of ministry in our church?

Not Effective   Very Effective

1   2   3   4   5   6   7   8   9   10

Personal notes (optional):

Building Relationships within the Body of Christ
through sharing our lives with one another.

How effective are we at living out this element of ministry in our church?

Not Effective   Very Effective

1   2   3   4   5   6   7   8   9   10

Personal notes (optional):

Building Relationships within the Body of Christ
through caring for one another.

How effective are we at living out this element of ministry in our church?

Not Effective   Very Effective

1   2   3   4   5   6   7   8   9   10

Personal notes (optional):

Building Relationships within the Body of Christ
through open communication.

How effective are we at living out this element of ministry in our church?

Not Effective   Very Effective

1   2   3   4   5   6   7   8   9   10

Personal notes (optional):

Building Relationships within the Body of Christ
through conflict resolution.

How effective are we at living out this element of ministry in our church?

Not Effective   Very Effective

1   2   3   4   5   6   7   8   9   10

Personal notes (optional):

Building Relationships within the Body of Christ
through forgiveness.

How effective are we at living out this element of ministry in our church?

Not Effective   Very Effective

1   2   3   4   5   6   7   8   9   10

Personal notes (optional):

Building Relationships within the Body of Christ
through healing.

How effective are we at living out this element of ministry in our church?

Not Effective   Very Effective

1   2   3   4   5   6   7   8   9   10

Personal notes (optional):

Building Relationships within the Body of Christ
through bearing one another's burdens.

How effective are we at living out this element of ministry in our church?

Not Effective   Very Effective

1   2   3   4   5   6   7   8   9   10

Personal notes (optional):

Acknowledging and Encouraging
great diversity within the body of Christ and teaching its members how to work together, disagree with love and respect, and creatively resolve conflicts.

How effective are we at living out this element of ministry in our church?

Not Effective   Very Effective

1   2   3   4   5   6   7   8   9   10

Personal notes (optional):

Overall Rating

How effective are we at living out this characteristic in our church (average score)?

Not Effective   Very Effective

1   2   3   4   5   6   7   8   9   10

Personal notes (optional):

A Commitment to Loving and Caring Relationships

1. *What* are we doing to live out this characteristic today? At present what are our strengths? What are we doing well?

2. *Where* do we want to be in the characteristic "A Commitment to Loving and Caring Relationships" in the next year or two? What is our *dream* for the future?

3. *How* will we get where we want to be in living out "A Commitment to Loving and Caring Relationships" in the next year or two?

Servant-Leadership Development

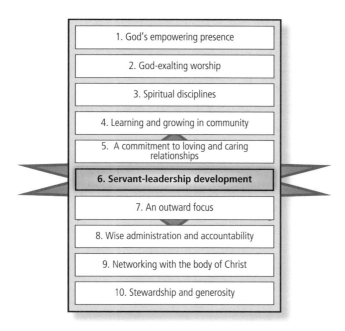

1. God's empowering presence
2. God-exalting worship
3. Spiritual disciplines
4. Learning and growing in community
5. A commitment to loving and caring relationships
6. Servant-leadership development
7. An outward focus
8. Wise administration and accountability
9. Networking with the body of Christ
10. Stewardship and generosity

The healthy church identifies and develops individuals whom God has called and given the gift of leadership and challenges them to be servant-leaders.

For church government, the healthy church:

- is led by persons who understand the church's vision, communicate it clearly to the congregation, and organize the body and each of its ministry groups so that the vision becomes reality

- motivates potential leaders by challenging them to serve for the glory of God
- develops a sense of collegiality among leaders, both lay and clergy
- encourages turnover yet stability in lay leadership
- evaluates the church's effectiveness, manages change, and plans for the future
- seeks to unify the congregation behind its leaders

For ministry leadership, the healthy church:

- creates an environment in which men and women with ministry gifts are developed to serve as servant-leaders
- encourages ministries to be led by laypersons as much as possible
- makes sure that ministry leadership is shared widely among congregation members
- works hard to assure that laypersons are partners who are respected, honored, mobilized, and freed to minister both inside and outside the church
- equips and empowers others to serve in ministry

From him [Christ] the whole body, joined and held together by every supporting ligament, grows and builds itself up in love, as each part does its work.

Ephesians 4:16

The following Scriptures from Jesus' life and teaching relate to servant-leadership development. Reflect on them before evaluating your church on this characteristic.

Matthew 8:5–13 *The centurion replied, "Lord, I do not deserve to have you come under my roof. But just say the word, and my servant will be healed"* (v. 8).
When Jesus heard this, he . . . said . . . "I tell you the truth, I have not found anyone in Israel with such great faith" (v. 10).

Matthew 18:4–5 *Therefore, whoever humbles himself like this child is the greatest in the kingdom of heaven. And whoever welcomes a little child like this in my name welcomes me.*

Matthew 20:26–28 *Whoever wants to become great among you must be your servant, and whoever wants to be first must be your slave* (vv. 26–27).

Matthew 23:11–12 *The greatest among you will be your servant. For whoever exalts himself will be humbled, and whoever humbles himself will be exalted.*

John 13:4–17 *Now that I, your Lord and Teacher, have washed your feet, you also should wash one another's feet. I have set you an example that you should do as I have done for you. I tell you the truth, no servant is greater than his master, nor is a messenger greater than the one who sent him* (vv. 14–16).

Parable of the Faithful and Wise Servant: Matthew 24:45–51 *Who then is the faithful and wise servant, whom the master has put in charge of the servants in his household to give them their food at the proper time? It will be good for that servant whose master finds him doing so when he returns* (vv. 45–46).

Parable of the Watchful Servants: Luke 12:35–38 *Be dressed ready for service and keep your lamps burning, like men waiting for their master to return from a wedding banquet. . . . It will be good for those servants whose master finds them watching when he comes. . . . he will dress himself to serve, will have them recline at the table and will come and wait on them* (vv. 35–37).

Parable of the Lowest Seat at the Feast: Luke 14:7–11 *But when you are invited, take the lowest place, so that when your host comes, he will say to you, "Friend, move up to a better place." Then you will be honored in the presence of all your fellow guests. For everyone who exalts himself will be humbled, and he who humbles himself will be exalted* (vv. 10–11).

Assess your church in regard to its health in these areas:

The Church Is Led
by persons who understand the church's vision, communicate it clearly to the congregation, and organize the body and each of its ministry groups so that the vision becomes reality.

How effective are we at living out this element of leadership in our church?

Not Effective   Very Effective

1   2   3   4   5   6   7   8   9   10

Personal notes (optional):

The Church Motivates
potential leaders by challenging them to serve for the glory of God.

How effective are we at living out this element of leadership in our church?

Not Effective   Very Effective

1   2   3   4   5   6   7   8   9   10

Personal notes (optional):

The Church Develops
a sense of collegiality among leaders, both lay and clergy.

How effective are we at living out this element of leadership in our church?

Not Effective   Very Effective

1   2   3   4   5   6   7   8   9   10

Personal notes (optional):

The Church Encourages
turnover yet stability in lay leadership.

How effective are we at living out this element of leadership in our church?

Not Effective   Very Effective

1   2   3   4   5   6   7   8   9   10

Personal notes (optional):

The Church Evaluates
the church's effectiveness, manages change, and plans for the future.

How effective are we at living out this element of leadership in our church?

Not Effective   Very Effective

1   2   3   4   5   6   7   8   9   10

Personal notes (optional):

The Church Seeks
to unify the congregation behind its leaders.

How effective are we at living out this element of leadership in our church?

Not Effective   Very Effective

1   2   3   4   5   6   7   8   9   10

Personal notes (optional):

The Church Creates
an environment in which men and women with ministry gifts are developed to serve as servant-leaders.

How effective are we at living out this element of leadership in our church?

Not Effective   Very Effective

1   2   3   4   5   6   7   8   9   10
Personal notes (optional):

The Church Works Hard
to assure that laypersons are partners who are respected, honored, mobilized, and freed to minister both inside and outside the church.

How effective are we at living out this element of leadership in our church?

Not Effective   Very Effective

1   2   3   4   5   6   7   8   9   10
Personal notes (optional):

The Church Encourages
ministries to be led by laypersons as much as possible.

How effective are we at living out this element of leadership in our church?

Not Effective   Very Effective

1   2   3   4   5   6   7   8   9   10
Personal notes (optional):

The Church Equips and Empowers
others to serve in ministry.

How effective are we at living out this element of leadership in our church?

Not Effective   Very Effective

1   2   3   4   5   6   7   8   9   10
Personal notes (optional):

The Church Makes Sure That Ministry Leadership
is shared widely among congregation members.

How effective are we at living out this element of leadership in our church?

Not Effective   Very Effective

1   2   3   4   5   6   7   8   9   10
Personal notes (optional):

Overall Rating
How effective are we at living out this characteristic in our church (average score)?

Not Effective   Very Effective

1   2   3   4   5   6   7   8   9   10
Personal notes (optional):

Servant-Leadership Development

1. *What* are we doing to live out this characteristic today? At present what are our strengths? What are we doing well?

2. *Where* do we want to be in the characteristic "Servant-Leadership Development" in the next year or two? What is our *dream* for the future?

3. *How* will we get where we want to be in living out "Servant-Leadership Development" in the next year or two?

An Outward Focus

The healthy church places high priority on communicating the truth of Jesus and demonstrating the love of Jesus to those outside the faith.

1. God's empowering presence
2. God-exalting worship
3. Spiritual disciplines
4. Learning and growing in community
5. A commitment to loving and caring relationships
6. Servant-leadership development
7. An outward focus
8. Wise administration and accountability
9. Networking with the body of Christ
10. Stewardship and generosity

Specifically, the church with an outward focus has a growing sense of the importance of outreach and:

- intentionally communicates the message of Christ in culturally relevant ways to those outside the family of God
- commits to the passing on of our faith to the next generation
- demonstrates to the world through acts of love, justice, and mercy that "God became flesh"
- welcomes and enfolds a steady stream of new people at all stages of their spiritual journey:
    - seeking nonbelievers
    - recent converts
    - enthusiastic young Christians
    - believers with questions, doubts, and struggles
    - active kingdom builders
    - wiser, older Christians
- experiments continually to find more effective ways to communicate the gospel to nonbelievers in the family, marketplace, community, and neighborhood
- develops a strategy for global awareness and international mission involvement

For the Son of Man came to seek and to save what was lost.

Luke 19:10

The following Scriptures from Jesus' life and teaching relate to communicating the truth of Jesus and demonstrating his love to those outside the faith. Reflect on them before evaluating your church on this characteristic.

Matthew 9:36–38 *When he saw the crowds, he had compassion on them. . . . Then he said to his disciples, "The harvest is plentiful but the workers are few. Ask the Lord of the harvest, therefore, to send out workers into his harvest field."*

Matthew 10:7–8 *As you go, preach this message: "The kingdom of heaven is near. Heal the sick, raise the dead, cleanse those who have leprosy, drive out demons. Freely you have received, freely give."*

Matthew 24:14 *And this gospel of the kingdom will be preached in the whole world as a testimony to all nations, and then the end will come.*

Matthew 28:18–20 *Go and make disciples of all nations, baptizing them in the name of the Father and of the Son and of the Holy Spirit, and teaching them to obey everything I have commanded you. And surely I am with you always, to the very end of the age (vv. 19–20).*

Luke 16:19–31 *Then I beg you, father, send Lazarus to my father's house, for I have five brothers. Let him warn them, so that they will not also come to this place of torment (vv. 27–28).*

Luke 19:10 *For the Son of Man came to seek and to save what was lost.*

Luke 24:45–47 *Repentance and forgiveness of sins will be preached in his name to all nations, beginning at Jerusalem (v. 47).*

John 1:41–42 *The first thing Andrew did was to find his brother Simon and tell him, "We have found the Messiah." . . . And he brought him to Jesus.*

John 17:20–21 *I pray also for those who will believe in me through their message, that all of them may be one, Father, just as you are in me and I am in you. May they also be in us so that the world may believe that you have sent me.*

Parable of the Sheep and the Goats: Matthew 25:31–46 *Then the righteous will answer him, "Lord, when did we see you hungry and feed you, or thirsty and give you something to drink? When did we see you a stranger and invite you in, or needing clothes and clothe you? When did we see you sick or in prison and go to visit you?"*

The King will reply, "I tell you the truth, whatever you did for one of the least of these brothers of mine, you did for me" (vv. 37–40).

Assess your church in regard to its health in the following areas:

Intentionally Communicating
the message of Christ in culturally relevant ways to those outside the family of God.

How effective are we at living out this element of ministry in our church?

Not Effective   Very Effective

1   2   3   4   5   6   7   8   9   10

Personal notes (optional):

Welcoming and Enfolding
a steady stream of new people at all stages of their spiritual journey.

How effective are we at living out this element of ministry in our church?

Not Effective   Very Effective

1   2   3   4   5   6   7   8   9   10

Personal notes (optional):

Committed
to the passing on of our faith to the next generation.

How effective are we at living out this element of ministry in our church?

Not Effective   Very Effective

1   2   3   4   5   6   7   8   9   10

Personal notes (optional):

Experimenting
continually to find more effective ways to communicate the gospel to nonbelievers in the family, marketplace, community, and neighborhood.

How effective are we at living out this element of ministry in our church?

Not Effective   Very Effective

1   2   3   4   5   6   7   8   9   10

Personal notes (optional):

Demonstrating
to the world through acts of love, justice, and mercy that "God became flesh."

How effective are we at living out this element of ministry in our church?

Not Effective   Very Effective

1   2   3   4   5   6   7   8   9   10

Personal notes (optional):

Developing
a strategy for global awareness and international missions involvement.

How effective are we at living out this element of ministry in our church?

Not Effective   Very Effective

1   2   3   4   5   6   7   8   9   10

Personal notes (optional):

Overall Rating

How effective are we at living out this characteristic in our church (average score)?

Not Effective   Very Effective

1   2   3   4   5   6   7   8   9   10

Personal notes (optional):

_____

An Outward Focus

1. *What* are we doing to live out this characteristic today? At present what are our strengths? What are we doing well?

2. *Where* do we want to be in the characteristic "An Outward Focus" in the next year or two? What is our *dream* for the future?

3. *How* will we get where we want to be in living out "An Outward Focus" in the next year or two?

Wise Administration and Accountability

The healthy church utilizes appropriate facilities, equipment, and systems to provide maximum support for the growth and development of its ministries.

1. God's empowering presence
2. God-exalting worship
3. Spiritual disciplines
4. Learning and growing in community
5. A commitment to loving and caring relationships
6. Servant-leadership development
7. An outward focus
8. Wise administration and accountability
9. Networking with the body of Christ
10. Stewardship and generosity

The healthy church fosters wise administration and accountability as it:

- strives for excellence, effectiveness, and efficiency through management practices that emphasize responsibility and accountability
- creates support systems to meet the functional needs of the ministry
- conducts an ongoing evaluation of church progress against its mission and vision
- develops a broad base of support among its members
- provides appropriately for its staff
- plans for the longevity of the ministry and for leadership transitions
- conducts an honest assessment of the strengths and weaknesses, opportunities and threats to its ministry
- thinks and acts strategically

So if you have not been trustworthy in handling worldly wealth, who will trust you with true riches?

Luke 16:11

The following Scriptures from Jesus' life and teaching relate to wise administration and accountability. Reflect on them before evaluating your church on this characteristic.

Mark 11:15–18 *He overturned the tables of the money changers and the benches of those selling doves, and would not allow anyone to carry merchandise through the temple courts* (vv. 15–16).

Luke 16:10–12 *Whoever can be trusted with very little can also be trusted with much, and whoever is dishonest with very little will also be dishonest with much. So if you have not been trustworthy in handling worldly wealth, who will trust you with true riches?* (vv. 10–11).

Luke 16:13 *No servant can serve two masters. Either he will hate the one and love the other, or he will be devoted to the one and despise the other. You cannot serve both God and Money.*

Luke 19:1–10 *But Zacchaeus stood up and said to the Lord, ". . . Here and now I give half of my possessions to the poor, and if I have cheated anybody out of anything, I will pay back four times the amount"* (v. 8).

Luke 20:21–25 *So the spies questioned him: "Teacher . . . Is it right for us to pay taxes to Caesar or not?"* (vv. 21–22).

He . . . said to them, "Show me a denarius. Whose portrait and inscription are on it?"

"Caesar's," they replied.

He said to them, "Then give to Caesar what is Caesar's, and to God what is God's" (vv. 23–25).

Parable of the Talents: Matthew 25:14–30 *Well done, good and faithful servant! You have been faithful with a few things; I will put you in charge of many things. Come and share your master's happiness!* (v. 23).

Parable of the Shrewd Manager: Luke 16:1–15 *Whoever can be trusted with very little can also be trusted with much, and whoever is dishonest with very little will also be dishonest with much. So if you have not been trustworthy in handling worldly wealth, who will trust you with true riches? And if you have not been trustworthy with someone else's property, who will give you property of your own?"* (vv. 10–12).

Assess your church in regard to its health in the following areas:

Striving
for excellence, effectiveness, and efficiency through management practices that emphasize responsibility and accountability.

How effective are we at living out this element of accountability in our church?

Not Effective   Very Effective

1   2   3   4   5   6   7   8   9   10

Personal notes (optional):

Creating
support systems to meet the functional needs of the ministry.

How effective are we at living out this element of administration in our church?

Not Effective   Very Effective

1   2   3   4   5   6   7   8   9   10

Personal notes (optional):

Conducting
an ongoing evaluation of church progress against its mission and vision.

How effective are we at living out this element of accountability in our church?

Not Effective   Very Effective

1   2   3   4   5   6   7   8   9   10

Personal notes (optional):

Developing
a broad base of support among its members.

How effective are we at living out this element of administration in our church?

Not Effective   Very Effective

1   2   3   4   5   6   7   8   9   10

Personal notes (optional):

Providing
appropriately for its staff.

How effective are we at living out this element of administration in our church?

Not Effective   Very Effective

1   2   3   4   5   6   7   8   9   10

Personal notes (optional):

Planning
for the longevity of the ministry and for leadership transitions.

How effective are we at living out this element of administration in our church?

Not Effective   Very Effective

1   2   3   4   5   6   7   8   9   10

Personal notes (optional):

Conducting
an honest assessment of the strengths and weaknesses, opportunities and threats to its ministry.

How effective are we at living out this element of accountability in our church?

Not Effective   Very Effective

1   2   3   4   5   6   7   8   9   10
Personal notes (optional):

Thinking and Acting Strategically
How effective are we at living out this element of administration in our church?

Not Effective   Very Effective

1   2   3   4   5   6   7   8   9   10
Personal notes (optional):

Overall Rating
How effective are we at living out this characteristic in our church (average score)?

Not Effective   Very Effective

1   2   3   4   5   6   7   8   9   10
Personal notes (optional):

Wise Administration and Accountability

1. *What* are we doing to live out this characteristic today? At present what are our strengths? What are we doing well?

2. *Where* do we want to be in the characteristic "Wise Administration and Accountability" in the next year or two? What is our *dream* for the future?

3. *How* will we get to where we want to be in living out "Wise Administration and Accountability" in the next year or two?

Networking with the Body of Christ

The healthy church reaches out to others in the body of Christ for collaboration, resource sharing, learning opportunities, and united celebrations of worship.

Networking with the body of Christ includes such things as:

1. God's empowering presence

2. God-exalting worship

3. Spiritual disciplines

4. Learning and growing in community

5. A commitment to loving and caring relationships

6. Servant-leadership development

7. An outward focus

8. Wise administration and accountability

9. Networking with the body of Christ

10. Stewardship and generosity

- pastors within the same town meeting regularly to pray for and encourage each other
- churches developing ministry specialties that meet the needs of their community without overlapping or competing with each other
- ministry leaders receiving training for their specific ministry with other leaders throughout the entire region
- area-wide celebrations where Christians join to worship God together and affirm their unity in Christ
- the gathering of the church in a variety of training and networking settings
- sharing resources between churches
- fostering interdependence across denominational boundaries
- communicating with one another through the use of new and effective technologies, such as the Internet

May they [the church] be brought to complete unity to let the world know that you sent me and have loved them even as you have loved me.

John 17:23

The following Scriptures from Jesus' life and teaching relate to reaching out to others in the body of Christ. Reflect on them before evaluating your church on this characteristic.

Luke 10:1–16 *The Lord appointed seventy-two others and sent them two by two ahead of him. . . . He told them . . . "He who listens to you listens to me; he who rejects you rejects me; but he who rejects me rejects him who sent me"* (vv. 1–2, 16).

Luke 10:38–42 *Mary . . . sat at the Lord's feet listening. . . . But Martha was distracted by all the preparations. . . . the Lord answered . . . "Mary has chosen what is better, and it will not be taken away from her"* (vv. 39–42).

Luke 22:19–20 *Do this in remembrance of me* (v. 19).

Luke 24:13–35 *As they talked . . . Jesus himself came up and walked along with them* (v. 15).

> *"Were not our hearts burning within us while he talked with us on the road and opened the Scriptures to us?"* (v. 32).

John 13:3–17 *You also should wash one another's feet. I have set you an example that you should do as I have done for you"* (vv. 14–15).

John 15:13–17 *Greater love has no one than this, that he lay down his life for his friends. . . . This is my command: Love each other* (vv. 13, 17).

John 17:22–23 *I have given them the glory that you gave me, that they may be one as we are one: I in them and you in me. May they be brought to complete unity to let the world know that you sent me and have loved them even as you have loved me.*

John 17:26 *I have made you known to them, and will continue to make you known in order that the love you have for me may be in them and that I myself may be in them.*

Parable of the Lamp: Matthew 5:14–16 *You are the light of the world. A city on a hill cannot be hidden. Neither do people light a lamp and put it under a bowl. Instead they put it on its stand, and it gives light to everyone in the house. In the same way, let your light shine before men, that they may see your good deeds and praise your Father in heaven.*

Assess your church in regard to its health in the following areas:

Our Pastor
and other pastors within the same town meet regularly to pray for each other.

How effective are we at living out this element of networking in our church?

Not Effective | Very Effective

1   2   3   4   5   6   7   8   9   10

Personal notes (optional):

Area-wide Celebrations
where Christians join to worship God together and affirm their unity in Christ.

How effective are we at living out this element of networking in our church?

Not Effective | Very Effective

1   2   3   4   5   6   7   8   9   10

Personal notes (optional):

Churches Develop
ministry specialties that meet the needs of our community without overlapping or competing with each other.

How effective are we at living out this element of networking in our church?

Not Effective | Very Effective

1   2   3   4   5   6   7   8   9   10

Personal notes (optional):

Gathering
of the church in a variety of training and networking settings.

How effective are we at living out this element of networking in our church?

Not Effective | Very Effective

1   2   3   4   5   6   7   8   9   10

Personal notes (optional):

Ministry Leaders Receive Training
for their specific ministry area with other leaders throughout the entire region.

How effective are we at living out this element of networking in our church?

Not Effective | Very Effective

1   2   3   4   5   6   7   8   9   10

Personal notes (optional):

Sharing
resources between churches.

How effective are we at living out this element of networking in our church?

Not Effective | Very Effective

1   2   3   4   5   6   7   8   9   10

Personal notes (optional):

Fostering Interdependence
across denominational boundaries.

How effective are we at living out this element of networking in our church?

Not Effective   Very Effective

1   2   3   4   5   6   7   8   9   10
Personal notes (optional):

Communicating
with one another through the use of new technologies such as the Internet.

How effective are we at living out this element of networking in our church?

Not Effective   Very Effective

1   2   3   4   5   6   7   8   9   10
Personal notes (optional):

Overall Rating
How effective are we at living out this characteristic in our church (average score)?

Not Effective   Very Effective

1   2   3   4   5   6   7   8   9   10
Personal notes (optional):

Networking with the Body of Christ

1. *What* are we doing to live out this characteristic today? At present what are our strengths? What are we doing well?

2. *Where* do we want to be in the characteristic "Networking with the Body of Christ" in the next year or two? What is our *dream* for the future?

3. *How* will we get to where we want to be in living out "Networking with the Body of Christ" in the next year or two?

Stewardship and Generosity

The healthy church teaches its members that they are stewards of their God-given resources and challenges them to be sacrificially generous in sharing with others.

The attitude of the leaders and members of the local church is a tangible expression of the attitude of Jesus, who taught that "from everyone who has been given much, much will be demanded; and from the one who has been entrusted with much, much more will be asked" (Luke 12:48) and "where your treasure is, there will your heart be also" (Matt. 6:21), and is evident in their:

- teaching on generosity and financial planning
- sharing facilities and programs with others
- giving a generous portion of the annual budget to local and international missions
- providing abundantly for those in need within the fellowship of believers, including the unemployed, the widowed, and single parents
- operating within the church's income, accounting for all contributions
- operating in accordance with the principles of the Evangelical Council for Financial Accountability or similar finanical accountability group

1. God's empowering presence

2. God-exalting worship

3. Spiritual disciplines

4. Learning and growing in community

5. A commitment to loving and caring relationships

6. Servant-leadership development

7. An outward focus

8. Wise administration and accountability

9. Networking with the body of Christ

10. Stewardship and generosity

Remember this: Whoever sows sparingly will also reap sparingly, and whoever sows generously will also reap generously.

2 Corinthians 9:6

The following Scriptures from Jesus' life and teaching relate to stewardship and generosity. Reflect on them before evaluating your church on this characteristic.

Matthew 6:19–21 *Do not store up for yourselves treasures on earth. . . . But store up for yourselves treasures in heaven. . . . For where your treasure is, there your heart will be also.*

Mark 12:41–44 *This poor widow has put more into the treasury than all the others. They all gave out of their wealth; but she, out of her poverty, put in everything—all she had to live on (vv. 43–44).*

Luke 6:30 *Give to everyone who asks you, and if anyone takes what belongs to you, do not demand it back.*

Luke 6:38 *Give, and it will be given to you. A good measure, pressed down, shaken together and running over, will be poured into your lap. For with the measure you use, it will be measured to you.*

Luke 12:15 *Watch out! Be on your guard against all kinds of greed; a man's life does not consist in the abundance of his possessions.*

Luke 12:32–34 *Do not be afraid, little flock, for your Father has been pleased to give you the kingdom. Sell your possessions and give to the poor (vv. 32–33).*

Luke 14:12–14 *But when you give a banquet, invite the poor, the crippled, the lame, the blind, and you will be blessed (vv. 13–14).*

Parable of the Rich Fool: Luke 12:16–21 *The ground of a certain rich man produced a good crop. He thought to himself, "What shall I do? I have no place to store my crops."*

Then he said . . . "I will tear down my barns and build bigger ones, and there I will store all my grain and my goods. And I'll say to myself, 'You have plenty of good things laid up for many years. Take life easy; eat, drink and be merry.'"

But God said to him, "You fool! This very night your life will be demanded from you. Then who will get what you have prepared for yourself?"

This is how it will be with anyone who stores up things for himself but is not rich toward God.

Assess your church in regard to its health in the following areas:

Teaching
on generosity and financial planning.

How effective are we at living out this element of stewardship in our church?

Not Effective   Very Effective

1   2   3   4   5   6   7   8   9   10

Personal notes (optional):

Providing
abundantly for those in need within the fellowship of believers, including the unemployed, the widowed, and single parents.

How effective are we at living out this element of stewardship and generosity in our church?

Not Effective   Very Effective

1   2   3   4   5   6   7   8   9   10

Personal notes (optional):

Sharing
facilities and programs with others.

How effective are we at living out this element of stewardship and generosity in our church?

Not Effective   Very Effective

1   2   3   4   5   6   7   8   9   10

Personal notes (optional):

Operating within the Church's Income
and accounting for all contributions.

How effective are we at living out this element of stewardship in our church?

Not Effective   Very Effective

1   2   3   4   5   6   7   8   9   10

Personal notes (optional):

Giving
a generous portion of the annual budget to local and international missions.

How effective are we at living out this element of stewardship and generosity in our church?

Not Effective   Very Effective

1   2   3   4   5   6   7   8   9   10

Personal notes (optional):

Operating in Accordance
with the principles of the Evangelical Council for Financial Accountability or similar financial accountability group.

How effective are we at living out this element of stewardship in our church?

Not Effective   Very Effective

1   2   3   4   5   6   7   8   9   10

Personal notes (optional):

Overall Rating

How effective are we at living out this characteristic in our church (average score)?

Not Effective   Very Effective

1   2   3   4   5   6   7   8   9   10

Personal notes (optional):

_____

Stewardship and Generosity

1. *What* are we doing to live out this characteristic today? At present what are our strengths? What are we doing well?

2. *Where* do we want to be in the characteristic "Stewardship and Generosity" in the next year or two? What is our *dream* for the future?

3. *How* will we get to where we want to be in living out "Stewardship and Generosity" in the next year or two?

Shortened Versions of Assessment Tools with Excel Tabulation Spreadsheet Software

Available from Vision New England (www .VisionNewEngland.com) are two short versions of healthy church assessment tools for leadership teams and congregations. They were designed for local churches to use with larger numbers of leaders and members who participate in the healthy church assessment process. You may wish to consider using these tools to broaden the scope of involvement and to deepen the commitment level of your church in assessing your church's vitality according to the Ten Characteristics of a Healthy Church.

Leadership Team Assessment Tool (short version)
Includes all the basic evaluative questions contained within section 2 of this workbook, Time for Dialogue and Assessment.

Congregational Assessment Tool (companion to Leadership Team Assessment Tool)
Designed to gain input from members of the congregation to enhance leadership team discussions as the church proceeds through the healthy church assessment process.

Part 3
Time for Planning

What Do We Do with What We've Learned?

Both during and subsequent to the dialogue and assessment phases, it is vitally important that you begin to interject elements of strategic thinking and planning that will lead you into future ministry pursuits clearly ordained by God. This is where the fun begins!

On a recent facilitation assignment at People's Baptist Church, a vibrant African American congregation in Boston, the planning flowed naturally out of nearly one year of their planning team's conversations. They had conducted extensive interviews with members of the congregation and leadership teams, collected nearly one hundred congregational assessment tools, prioritized their findings, and were poised to begin implementing goals that made sense to everyone involved in this process. As a result, they drafted five very well-articulated SMART (Specific, Measurable, Achievable, Results-oriented, Time-dated) goals that would compel them forward as a church. These five goals were accompanied by a detailed plan for each of the major ministries of the church. When I left the room on my final evening with them, I was excited to observe the energetic creativity of this gifted group of people. They worked hard, prayed diligently, sorted through a mountain of information, and were clearly focused on their next most logical steps for leading their church into the future.

I was reminded at that moment of the three most significant elements of the planning process. First of all, the most effective planning processes occur within the context of a *healthy team*, a team that functions well. To properly assess the health and vitality of the church, many people need to be involved in each stage of development. Second, the team needs to be led by a respected champion. This *church champion* is either the pastor or a respected lay leader, one who can maintain the discipline required to work through the process from A to Z. Third, the most important element of the experience is summarized in *empathetic listening*. When the leader and team make a conscious, genuine effort to hear from God, the congregation, and one another, the fruit that emerges is life-giving for all.

As you enter this next phase of *becoming a healthier church*, you will note the increased energy level emerging from your team. It is important to remind your team that this process is something that flows very naturally from God, the most effective of all strategic thinkers!

Why Plan?

When you consider this question for your church, it's important that you consider God's point of view! Is God a planning God, a strategic thinker; does he have a master plan in mind for his children; are we destined to discover our part in his plan? Some in your congregation may find the notion of planning very un-Christian or uninspired or inappropriate for the church to be involved in. So let's look to his Word and see if God gives us any hints about his view on this subject. Here are a few Scriptures to consider as we contemplate God's heart for planning.

- *Seek his plans with all your heart:* "'For I know the plans I have for you,' declares the LORD, 'plans to prosper you and not harm you, plans to give you hope and a future. Then you will call upon me and come and pray to me, and I will listen to you. You will seek me and find me when you seek me with all your heart. I will be found by you,' declares the LORD, 'and will bring you back from captivity. I will gather you from all the nations and places where I have banished you,' declares the LORD, 'and will bring you back to the place from which I carried you into exile'" (Jer. 29:11–14).

- *Seek his plans for the health of the body:* "Trust in the LORD with all your heart and lean not on your own understanding; in all your ways acknowledge him, and he will make your paths straight. Do not be wise in your own eyes; fear the LORD and shun evil. This will bring health to your body and nourishment to your bones" (Prov. 3:5–8).

- *Seek his plans with the wise counsel of others:* "Plans fail for lack of counsel, but with many advisers they succeed" (Prov. 15:22).

- *Seek his plans as one in spirit and purpose:* "If you have any encouragement from being united with Christ, if any comfort from his love, if any fellowship with the Spirit, if any tenderness and compassion, then make my joy complete by being like-minded, having the same love, being one in spirit and purpose" (Phil. 2:1–2).

- *Seek his plans to prepare God's people for service:* "It was he who gave some to be apostles, some to be prophets, some to be evangelists, and some to be pastors and teachers, to prepare God's people for works of service, so that the body of Christ may be built up until we all reach unity in the faith and in the knowledge of the Son of God and become mature, attaining to the whole measure of the fullness of Christ" (Eph. 4:11–13).

- *Seek his plans as good stewards of all that's entrusted to your care:* "Well done, good and faithful servant! You have been faithful with a few things; I will put you in charge of many things. Come and share your master's happiness!" (Matt. 25:23; see vv. 14–30).

- *Seek his plans so that you can know with certainty his mission:* "It would not be right for us to neglect the ministry of the word of God in order to wait on tables. . . . We will turn this responsibility over to them and will give our attention to prayer and the ministry of the word" (Acts 6:2–4; see vv. 1–7).

- *Seek his plans as you are led by the Holy Spirit:* "because those who are led by the Spirit of God are sons of God" (Rom. 8:14).

These are just a few places to turn to in the Word of God where it's apparent that God is indeed a strategic God and he delights to have his children discover his unique thumbprint for their individual lives and for their communities of faith. It's pure joy to know that God loves us enough to want to reveal his plans to us and he delights to empower us by his Spirit to know and fulfill his will. He doles out his will for us one little piece at a time. That's why it's important that we develop the planning discipline as his children. We need to know what is our "assigned task" (Mark 13:34) in the kingdom of God, and then wait on him in prayerful love and obedience to reveal his plan for us—one prayer, one day, one season, one year at a time. He wills to communicate and build an intimate relationship with his children so that we can know *his* heart's desire for our individual lives and our collective experience as the people of God. Celebrate the certainty of that truth today!

The Fruit of Discovery

One of my favorite Machiavelli (no relation to yours truly!) quotes is, "There is nothing more difficult to take in hand, more perilous to conduct, or more uncertain in its success than to take the lead in introducing a new order of things." It's true. Taking the lead in strategic planning for our lives—and the church—is hard work! But if you aim at nothing, you are certain to hit it every time. Discovering God's agenda for your church can become one of the most exhilarating experiences for your leadership team and congregation.

The goal is not the process of discovery but the fruit of discovery. The fruit of discovery is articulated in decisions that will move the whole or part toward a definite, clear outcome, which changes and enhances the way you accomplish your stated mission. Aiming in that direction will lead you to "hitting the target" of God's purposes for you—a goal worth pursuing.

Strategic planning, according to former president of InterVarsity Christian Fellowship, Steve Hayner, in a report to his board and staff several years ago, is *not:*

- the production of a detailed blueprint that's set in cement; it continually shifts over time
- the personal vision of one person; it needs to be a team-owned effort
- the work of planners; it requires leadership, a champion of the process (with planners to facilitate the process, input, tactics, etc.)
- something done once a year; it is integral to our daily life, ongoing, not occasional
- a way of eliminating risks; instead, it involves risk taking, entrepreneurial spirit, boldness, clarity about desired results
- the same as long-range planning, which in itself may or may not be strategic.

Hayner goes on to explain what strategic planning *is:*

- a process that helps leadership be active and positive rather than passive about their position in history
- action-oriented, concentrating on key decisions that will affect the future
- participatory and highly tolerant of controversy
- sensitive to the many elements that affect the success of a given strategy, such as:
  1. biblical/theological mandates
  2. the leading of the Holy Spirit
  3. traditions, values, and aspirations
  4. social, cultural, and environmental needs
  5. abilities and priorities of leadership
  6. institutional strengths and weaknesses
  7. special opportunities, resources, etc.

When you begin to see strategic planning as a friend rather than a foe, you will embrace the process with added energy and anticipation. The results of your shared labors of love will reveal themselves in the context of your ministry. Entering into this process with expectation that indeed God will bless and enlighten you along the way will certainly bring forth fruit that honors and pleases him!

Why the Resistance?

Even with such strong, compelling biblical evidence of God's blessing on a Spirit-empowered planning process, you will discover resistance to the process within yourself, your team, and your congregation. It exists for a variety of reasons. Which of the following apply to you?

We lack the discipline to maintain the process and see it to its most logical conclusion.

We lack experience in managing such a process within the context of a local church.

We lack faith in the process. We don't have an inner peace and security that planning is okay to do. We wonder, *Are we really trusting in God if we engage in planning?*

We lack resources and basic know-how in leading others through a new experience such as this.

We lack accountability for keeping the process alive and bringing it to helpful decisions that will impact the life of the church.

We tend to resist change—of any kind—and that mind-set aborts any constructive efforts to engage in this process at any meaningful level.

We fear a change may need to occur that will result in the loss of one of our most cherished activities.

We perceive planning as a worldly intrusion into the church that should be discouraged from every angle.

We lack the courage to walk into the planning process ready to listen, learn, and change.

It's important to acknowledge whatever resistance you face and prayerfully overcome that resistance with confidence in the process and the fruit of your labor.

Common Pitfalls of Planning

In New England the roads we drive on are generally horrible! The potholes are in abundance on most side roads. Some can be avoided, but you come on others so quickly, they are difficult to miss. On the road to church health, especially on the avenue called planning, it's important to know in advance which potholes—or pitfalls—to avoid. There are several possibilities to consider.

Making Planning Too Complex

The first common pitfall is when you *make the planning too complex*. In reality there are usually two or three key issues that will be discovered, and, if acted on appropriately, will lead to enhanced health and vitality. People's Baptist Church in Boston narrowed their planning down to revising their organizational chart, enhancing their community life, and streamlining their ministry priorities. When these issues were tackled, the goals for day-to-day ministry were delegated to each of the ministry teams where the specific plans were hammered out, goals were rewritten for greater ownership, and then each team implemented and evaluated its ministry.

Not Arriving at a Plan

Another pitfall is when you *don't reach conclusions and make an action plan*. If you don't tie up loose ends all along the way, with appropriate action steps outlined, then the nebulous nature of the experience will overshadow any productivity you sought to achieve. Coming to conclusions together is a great team-building exercise, no matter the size or composition of the group. On the other hand, if you make an action plan without first coming to conclusions, the team may choose a new direction that can be more difficult to untangle farther down the road.

Failure to Produce a Compelling Plan

If the *action plan that's created isn't simple and compelling*, then the whole experience becomes counterproductive. One church I worked with

had such a long document, with dozens of goals and action steps, that its complexity alone was overwhelming and was met with nonapproval because it appeared impossible to achieve. The objective here is to create a plan, the basic components of which each member can articulate without having to refer to the written document.

Failure to Revise the Plan

A common pitfall to planning is found further along in the process when you *don't revisit and revise the plan.* You need to remember that the plan is not to be cemented permanently. It needs to be fluid and adjustable along the way, revised and renewed according to the needs and resources available to you. Keep your planning documents alive—don't shelve them, file them, or even formalize them to the extent that they become too permanent and, ultimately, archived for later consideration. At Vision New England we hold our plans loosely, in more of a "white paper" format, with lots of room for give-and-take each step of the way.

Planning That's Too Long

Letting the process *take too long* is yet another pitfall to avoid. If you let the planning cycle go on and on endlessly, your team will tire of the experience and will begin to mumble and complain about the value of continuing or repeating this in the future. Part of the discipline in planning is keeping the group moving forward, stretching them without breaking them, and continuously reminding them of the goals you are seeking to achieve. As you successfully achieve unity of purpose, keep the group moving forward toward conclusion and celebration.

Not Listening to God

Finally, the most significant pitfall to avoid is *not listening enough to God and instead trusting your own instincts* about the future direction of your church. The most successful planning processes bring the group toward agreement on the big picture of where you are heading, even if the details are not ironed out or fully agreed on. It's important that you strive as a team to lean fully in God's direction to hear his voice, resonate with his heart, understand his will, and trust his empowering presence to lead, guide, and direct you toward the fulfillment of his glory being revealed in and through you as his children.

Strategic planning is a process that God through his Holy Spirit must direct. Become a people of prayer as you trust him for his design for your church.

Almighty God, you are wise in all your ways and patient in all your dealings with your children. You are the potter, we are the clay; mold us and make us to reflect your radiant splendor throughout our days of service here on earth. We want to be wise in all of our dealings with one another, in all of our planning for the future, in all of our responsible acts of leadership and oversight of the ministries you have called us to serve. Teach us what it means to trust you as we manage the changes that come our way. Love us as we assess and evaluate ourselves and one another— may this be affirming and building for all. Give us a renewed sense of our accountability first and foremost to you, and secondarily to each other as brothers and sisters in Christ. Help us dream big dreams for you and your kingdom and set realistic goals for accomplishing what you have destined for us to do. In all ways and in every day, keep us in the center of your will, held securely in the palms of your loving hands. Our love for you continues to grow with each succeeding day. Refresh and renew us in our love and service. For your name's sake. Amen.

Seven Planning Questions

Some church leaders find planning a formidable exercise. In reality the planning process is very simple—*conceptually*. It can be described by a series of seven key questions that need to be answered by every leadership team. Getting your team to agree on the answers to these questions may or may not be so simple, depending on the specific circumstances and the health of the relationships of leaders in your church. The strategic plans you agree on together—under the leadership of the Holy Spirit—will shape your church's effectiveness in the months ahead. It's worth the effort—guaranteed!

The seven major questions that must be answered by you and your church leaders are:

1. *Spiritual Needs Assessment*
   What are the greatest spiritual needs of our church and our community?
2. *Strengths and Weaknesses*
   What are the greatest strengths and weakness of our church?
3. *Opportunities and Threats or Barriers*
   What are the most significant ministry opportunities for and potential threats (or barriers) to our church, given the answers to the first two questions?
4. *Ministry Options*
   What appear to be the most viable options for strengthening the ministry of our church?
5. *Ministry Platform*
   What is the primary ministry platform on which our specific ministries should be built? Included in the ministry platform are statement of faith, vision statement, mission statement, philosophy of ministry, and ministries.

6. *Ministry Goals*
   What goals is the Holy Spirit leading us to strive for to enhance our church's ministry over the next year? the next two to three years?
7. *Action Steps*
   What action steps must we accomplish to achieve these goals?

Questions 2, 3, and 4 are the primary focus of the healthy church assessment exercises given at the beginning of this workbook. If you have not completed the healthy church assessment tool, these questions must still be answered to adequately participate in the full planning process.

Each of these seven questions forms a step in the planning process. The process can be depicted rather simply in the following diagram.

Spiritual Needs Assessment
Strengths and Weaknesses
Opportunities and Threats or Barriers
Ministry Options
Ministry Platform
Ministry Goals
Action Steps

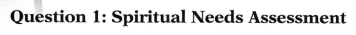

Question 1: Spiritual Needs Assessment

What are the greatest spiritual needs of our church and our community?

Guidelines

- Talk to lots of people outside your planning group to answer this question.
- In fact many community leaders can shed light on certain aspects of this question. Seek their opinions.
- The purpose of asking this question is to describe the spiritual climate or spiritual environment in which your church is seeking to minister.
- Recognize that many physical, emotional, intellectual, and economic needs have a spiritual component. We as Christians are called to minister to the whole person.
- Refer to demographic information from the most recent census. Most of this information is available on the Internet for your review and prayerful consideration.

Specific Questions

1. What is the history of our congregation? What were we initially called forth to do in our original charter? What did we inherit in this generation from previous ones?

   This is often the best place to begin when assessing the spiritual needs of your community. A lot can be learned by reviewing church records, annual meeting minutes, and other historical documents. Go back as far as possible to capture the essence of your church's "story line." The goal in researching this historical profile is a contextualized perspective!

   The research you do on your church and community should include:
   - Archival search—through the records you secure and review
   - Interviewing—asking as many questions of as many people as possible
   - Intercession—seeking the counsel of those who have been praying for your local church and community for years. What is their take on the spiritual condition of your ministry context?

2. What types of issues are unchurched people citing as the most common problems facing them or their friends and acquaintances? For example:
   - rebellious teenagers
   - high divorce rates
   - long working hours
   - lack of meaning in life
   - alcoholism and drug abuse
   - homelessness
   - vandalism

3. What specific people groups seem to be in the greatest need? For example:
   - single mothers
   - specific ethnic groups
   - teenagers

- retirees
- children
- factory workers

4. Which groups of people or which issues are not being effectively ministered to by any church in our neighborhood?
5. What is the demographic profile of our community in terms of:
    - age
    - marital status
    - education
    - type of employment
    - ethnic origin
    - church affiliation
    - household income
6. Rank the top needs of our church and community in descending order of importance.

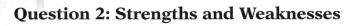

Question 2: Strengths and Weaknesses

Be sure to refer to your dialogue and assessment activities to inform this part of the planning process!

What are the greatest strengths and weaknesses of our church?

Guidelines

- Celebrate your church's strengths. Be upbeat about the positive aspects.
- Don't be too hard on yourselves for the weaknesses of your church. No congregation is called to offer all possible ministries. Only the church universal is the complete body of Christ.
- While no two churches are called to be alike, it is, however, important that each church achieve a minimum level of proficiency in each of the Ten Characteristics of a Healthy Church. All ten characteristics are important.
- The exact level of proficiency needed as a minimum must be decided by your church.

Specific Questions

1. What strengths and weaknesses were highlighted through the assessment process?
2. On which aspects of church life did your planning committee agree as either strengths or weaknesses?
3. In what areas did you disagree?
4. If there are areas of sharp disagreement, why is there a difference of opinion? Are there unspoken issues beneath the surface that haven't been openly acknowledged?

5. Which areas of weakness must be improved soon? For which areas can we take more time to make improvements?
6. Rank the top problem areas in order of importance, listing the one needing the most urgent attention first.

Question 3: Opportunities and Threats or Barriers

Be sure to refer to your dialogue and assessment activities to inform this part of the planning process!

What are the most significant ministry opportunities for and potential threats to our church, given the answers to the first two questions?

Guidelines

- Plan to devote most of your energy addressing needs that play to your strengths.
- Plan to devote a lesser amount of time strengthening your weaknesses.
- Remember, many people typically overestimate what they can do in one year and underestimate what they can do in five years or ten years.

Specific Questions

1. Which of the biggest needs in our community and our church could we seek to meet within one year? within three years? within five years?
2. Realistically, how many new ministries can our church launch at the same time?
3. How many existing ministries can we realistically expand or improve?
4. Are there any threats so severe that they could seriously harm our current ministry? Which threats? How could they do great harm?
5. Could any of the threats prevent our church from expanding or enhancing our current ministry? Which threats? How?
6. Which ministries should be discontinued, because of either the changing culture or inadequate leadership?

Question 4: Ministry Options

Be sure to refer to your dialogue and assessment activities to inform this part of the planning process!

What appear to be the most viable options for strengthening the ministry of our church?

Guidelines

- It is rare that there is only one possible way to strengthen a church's ministry.
- Give yourself some time to consider different alternatives.
- Ask the Holy Spirit to guide this critical process of considering different alternatives.

Specific Questions

1. What appear to be the most likely options for proactively pursuing new ministries?
2. How many ministries can be started simultaneously or how should they be phased in over time?
3. What weak areas must we improve to avoid hindering the future ministry?
4. How much change can our congregation adjust to in one year? in three years? in five years?

Once these first four questions are fully addressed in a team or group context, you are ready to move forward into the design of your ministry platform, specific goals, and action steps for becoming a healthy church. The first four questions form the bedrock to build on in continuing an effective planning process for improving the health of your church!

Question 5: Ministry Platform

What is the primary ministry platform on which our specific ministries should be built? What is the DNA of our church?

Before attempting to complete your ministry platform, it is essential that your leadership team spend considerable time individually and collectively in Bible study and prayer. Developing an effective ministry platform for your church requires that you have first heard from the Lord about his intentions for you. Some of the questions below will be easier than others to answer. Being united in the Spirit of God will enhance your experience and provide the insight necessary to determine these foundational issues. The skill to develop is listening—*to God and to one another. As you participate in Bible study and prayer times, both individually and collectively, listen for God's voice. What is he saying to you about your current and future ministry? Answer this question as you complete your ministry platform.*

Developing a ministry platform is the process of understanding God's unique design for your church and includes five key areas:

1. *Statement of Faith*—the doctrinal position of your church founded on God's Word. What is your doctrinal statement of faith upon which every aspect of your ministry hinges?

2. *Vision Statement*—the specific view of a preferred future based on your calling. This is like painting a picture of what you hope your future will become. Based on what you believe the Holy Spirit is calling your unique community of believers to be and do, what is the realistically attainable, although exceedingly difficult, vision for your church?
3. *Mission Statement*—the philosophical statement of your general, more global purpose—who you are and what you do to fulfill your vision. What do you believe God wills for you to do and for whom?
4. *Philosophy of Ministry Statement*—the description of how your commitments and attitudes shape how your church will execute your vision and mission. How does the fulfillment of your passion for ministry live itself out in the kind of people you intend to become? How proactively do you choose to serve together in fulfilling your shared ministry agenda? What are the spiritual and philosophical underpinnings that inspire you to love and action?
5. *Ministries*—the specific listing of ministries that will be utilized for executing your worship, fellowship, caring, service, and outreach. What ministries are essential in your pursuit of becoming a healthier church?

"For I know the plans I have for you," declares the Lord, "plans to prosper you and not to harm you, plans to give you hope and a future. Then you will call upon me and come and pray to me, and I will listen to you. You will seek me and find me when you seek me with all your heart."

Jeremiah 29:11–13

Trust in the Lord with all your heart
    and lean not on your own understanding;
in all your ways acknowledge him,
    and he will make your paths straight.
Do not be wise in your own eyes;
    fear the Lord and shun evil.
This will bring health to your body
    and nourishment to your bones.

Proverbs 3:5–8

Every Christian organization [and local church] must have a "ministry platform" if it is to be effective and truly accountable to God. The ministry platform will inform how decisions are made, goals are determined, and success is measured.

Becoming a Healthy Church, p. 165

Vision New England's Ministry Platform is spelled out in full detail in Becoming a Healthy Church, *pages 226–31 and serves as a model to review as you complete your own ministry platform.* You will note in this extensive ministry platform that a few additional issues are included, such as core beliefs, core values, strategy, and ministry profile. These are suggested areas for you to consider as complementary to the five key areas outlined above.

The following guidelines and samples are provided as an encouragement to your team. These are real samples from a variety of churches, but given anonymously so as to maintain purity in the exercise of developing your own similar statements. Please do not simply copy any of the ideas below. The creative exercise you and your team will experience by developing your own will reap far greater fruit!

Sample Vision Statements

1. To become a church that makes Jesus smile!
2. To become a Christian community where people are excited to participate in every aspect of our shared life and ministry.
3. To become a caring community, cultivating contagious Christians who are committed to the cause of Christ.
4. To become a biblically functioning community.
    Please note: For comparative purposes, the above four vision statements and the first four mission statements below are from the same four churches respectively.
5. To be a beacon of love, hope, and truth in Jesus Christ to our city and the world.
6. To be a regional church that introduces one thousand people into a personal relationship with, and a lifetime of obedience to, the Lord Jesus Christ.

Suggested characteristics of a good Vision Statement:

1. A good Vision Statement pictures the future of your church as you pray it will be.
2. A good Vision Statement describes the results you hope to realize in the "real world."
3. A good Vision Statement captures a bit of the uniqueness that you believe God has given to your church and its role in the broader kingdom of God.
4. A good Vision Statement is relatively short in length.
5. A good Vision Statement is compelling; that is, it serves as a motivational statement for church members.
6. A good Vision Statement is easy to memorize.

If you could start from scratch, how would you word your church's vision statement?

Sample Mission Statements

1. To serve God, one another, and the seeker with heartfelt love and enthusiasm.
2. To become a church where every member is engaged in worship, learning, fellowship, caring, and service.
3. To worship our God (Luke 4:8), evangelize our world (Matt. 28:19–20), and disciple one another to Christian maturity (Eph. 4:11–16).
4. To turn irreligious people into fully devoted followers of Jesus Christ.
5. To bring people to Jesus and membership in his family, develop them to Christ-like maturity, and equip them for their ministry in the church and life mission in the world, in order to magnify God's name.

6. We are to glorify God by responding to the Lord Jesus Christ through:
   Exalting him as Creator, Savior, and Lord
   Exemplifying him and the values of his kingdom
   Evangelizing his world
   Encompassing the past
   Enriching the culture

7. To be a church, gifted by the Holy Spirit, united in the love of Christ, touching God the Father in prayer and in worship, reflecting biblical truth with integrity, living in holiness, evangelizing the world.

8. Our cell-based church exists to exalt the Lord Jesus Christ, rejoicing in him as we bring believers to maturity, draw people to Jesus, equip them to serve, and become a reconciling force in the body of Christ.

Suggested characteristics of a good Mission Statement:

1. A good Mission Statement describes something about the purpose you believe your church should adopt as part of the larger body of Christ.
2. A good Mission Statement hints at how you hope to make your vision become reality under God's guidance.
3. A good Mission Statement is relatively short in length.
4. A good Mission Statement is compelling; that is, it serves as a motivational statement for church members.
5. A good Mission Statement is easy to memorize.

If you could start from scratch, how would you word your church's mission statement?

Sample Philosophy of Ministry Statements

1. We will:
   - maintain an unqualified, unconditional commitment to one another
   - empower leaders and ministry teams to serve in every aspect of our shared ministry
   - lovingly work with and challenge one another in our personal spiritual development
   - tirelessly pursue excellence
   - encourage creativity and freedom
   - be proactive and affirming
   - provide urgent forward movement to renewing joy in every aspect of life and service
   - unite around our commonly shared vision and mission
   - create ministries that serve the real needs of our congregation and community

2. We believe and are committed to:
   - effective biblical teachings
   - culturally relevant ministries
   - authenticity

- unified body of servants
- the truth that lost people matter to God
- Christ's followers must manifest their spiritual gifts
- loving relationships should permeate church life
- life change is enhanced in small groups
- excellence honors God and inspires people
- churches are led by those with leadership gifts

3. All believers are called by God to minister to him in prayer and in worship and to live out their faith in service of their fellow believers, their local community, and the world at large. Every believer is a minister and is equipped by God with gifts and talents for this purpose. The church is charged by God to care for believers' lives and to prepare them to minister through the discovery, development, and implementation of their gifts and talents. The leadership of the church should facilitate this process by developing and maintaining effective ministries and by preserving focus and order throughout all ministry activities.

4. We are committed to:
   - directing ourselves to the life-changing needs of the community
   - working toward leading people through a journey to faith and to reach their full potential
   - consistent prayer and worship, realizing it as an important element in spiritual growth
   - providing teaching, preaching, and leadership that points people toward Christ-likeness
   - becoming "other-centered" by centering on God and not ourselves
   - working with other churches to accomplish the expansion of the kingdom of God
   - accepting people where they are, believing they are valued, caring for them when hurt, desiring the best for them, erasing their offenses, and focusing them on Christ's love
   - accepting people into a loving environment where people can receive comfort
   - providing an atmosphere where people can listen and question and then discern the love of God
   - providing a safe place where people can hear and see the love and joy of God
   - bringing comfort to the brokenhearted
   - strengthening families

Suggested Characteristics of Philosophy of Ministry Statements:

1. A Philosophy Statement describes what people should experience if they join the church.
2. A Philosophy Statement captures a bit of the uniqueness that you believe God has given to your church in its role in the broader kingdom of God.
3. A Philosophy Statement articulates the way in which values and beliefs are lived out in the ministry context.

If you could start from scratch, how would you word your church's philosophy of ministry statement?

Question 6: Ministry Goals

What goals is the Holy Spirit leading us to strive for to enhance our church's ministry over the next year? the next two to three years?

Why Set Goals?

1. Goals concentrate our energy and attention.
2. Goals move us toward specific accomplishment.
3. Goals inspire greater effort than they articulate.
4. Goals provide a basis for periodic evaluation.
5. Goals can bring discipline into our life together.
6. Goals encourage consistency and stability.

When you don't do goal setting, you end up doing problem solving!

SMART goals are the qualitative and quantitative objectives that you believe God would have you strive to accomplish. They are the tangible ways that you will measure ministry effectiveness and monitor your planning process in fulfillment of your overall ministry strategy.

In your goal setting, make sure your goals are SMART:

Specific

Measurable

Achievable

Results-oriented

Time-dated

After writing your goals, measure them against the SMART acronym. Look at the goal and ask: Is this goal specific? Is it measurable? Is it achievable? Does it reflect a result we hope to accomplish? Is it time-dated so that we can evaluate its completion? If you could not answer yes to each of these questions, then the goal needs to be revised accordingly. On the other hand, if you are able to answer in the affirmative to all of these five basic questions, then you have achieved the objective of writing a SMART goal. Congratulations!

Samples of SMART Goals

Sample 1

To identify three to five key youth ministry strategic planning initiatives, by September 1, 2002, that will enhance our ministry to youth in our church and community.

Sample 2

To provide a once-a-week Bible study, prayer and share time for adult singles, to help each person grow spiritually and learn life application, beginning September 1, 2002.

Sample 3

To create three to five new small groups for young couples, by the end of this ministry year, that will build relationships and nurture Christ-like living.

Sample 4

To enhance our church's presence in the community by creating a public relations campaign plan by December 31, 2002.

Question 7: Action Steps

What action steps must we accomplish to achieve these goals?
Specific questions to address:

- What resources are needed to implement these goals? For example:
    - paid staff and/or volunteers
    - facilities and equipment
    - operating supplies
    - outside advice or guidance
    - training for new ministry leaders
    - leaders for the new ministry
- What will these resources cost?
- How can these resources be phased in?
- List in a table a simple step-by-step process to accomplish the ministry goals that includes:
    - *Why* we do *what* by *when.*
    - *How* we do it, *where,* and with *whom.*
- How should we turn these goals into SMART (Specific, Measurable, Achievable, Results-oriented, Time-dated) goals?

SMART Goals Worksheet

Staff Member/Group Name: _____

Ministry Year: _____ – _____

Think:	*Who*	*When*	*How*	*When*
What, Where, Why	*Leader/Helpers*	*Begin by*	*Resources Needed*	*Completed by*
Goal:				
Action Steps:				
1.				
2.				
3.				
4.				
5.				
6.				
Goal:				
Action Steps:				
1.				
2.				
3.				
4.				
5.				
6.				

Sample 1

SMART goal: To identify three to five key youth ministry strategic planning initiatives, by September 1, 2002, that will enhance our ministry to youth in our church and community.

Action Steps:

- Establish strategy design team of 6 to 8 youth, parents, and volunteers.
- Plan a six-month event schedule.
- Develop "Builders"—a small-group ministry for youth.
- Plan a short-term missions trip.
- Develop a "Parenting Your Teens" seminar.
- Hire a part-time junior high youth ministry associate.

Sample 2

SMART goal: To provide a once-a-week Bible study, prayer and share time for adult singles, to help each person grow spiritually and learn life application, beginning September 1, 2002.

Action Steps:

- Develop a council within the group to plan and implement the ministry. This council would consist of coordinators for prayer, outreach, contact, activities, and music.
- (Name) and (Name) would meet with the council regularly to support, encourage, and hold accountable the council members.
- Seek specific ideas for ways to minister and serve those within our group, the church, and our community.
- Network with other singles groups in our region.

Sample 3

SMART goal: To create three to five new small groups for young couples, by the end of this ministry year, that will build relationships and nurture Christ-like living.

Action Steps:

- Select possible study materials for the groups to use.
- Expand the small-group ministry by adding two groups in the fall and prepare to add others in January.
- Create a leaders' training group.
- Encourage the continued effectiveness of existing groups through the assistance of the pastor and the small-groups ministry council.

Sample 4

SMART goal: To enhance our church's presence in the community by creating a public relations campaign plan by December 31, 2002.

Action Steps:

- Design a new logo and related materials within.
- Establish a creative writing team for publications.
- Schedule the publishing of ministry brochures for major areas of ministry.
- Pray regularly for our community leaders and invite them to special programs.
- Create a two-year schedule of planned conferences and seminars.
- Expand the information on the web page.
- Develop a manual or guide for use by ministry teams in preparing to host a major event.
- Produce in-house videos for training, conferences, testimonies, and special-event coverage.

Mastering the Planning Cycle

After a church has gone through the step-by-step planning process, it is extremely important and useful to assess progress against goals on an annual basis. The time required to go through the process on subsequent occasions is considerably shorter than the first time. Every few years it is useful to conduct a more extended strategic planning process to help the leaders and the entire church think outside the box and be open to new directives from God.

It's important for pastors and church leaders to consider the seasons of the planning cycle:

Spring: Review prior year and begin developing strategy for year ahead.
- Do performance evaluations with review and revision of job description(s) for staff.
- Review and revise Ministry Platform.
- Write new SMART goals, with related action steps.
- Determine budget, calendar, and any additional team or personnel needs.

Summer: Finalize all planning details.
- Create ministry brochures to reflect new initiatives.
- Complete annual reports highlighting the previous year of ministry.

Fall: Implement plans; revise accordingly.

Winter: Mid-year checkups and adjustments.

Throughout the ministry year, it's important that ongoing contact with team members occurs so that there are no big surprises when it comes time to evaluate personnel and programs each spring. Through team meetings, one-on-one accountability and encouragement sessions, and regular written reports, the flow of communication is maintained. As a result, the quality of relationships is enhanced and the fruitfulness of ministry is multiplied.

This planning cycle is repeated year after year, thus reinforcing the disciplines of dialogue, assessment, and planning!

Guidelines for Leaders on Change Management, Accountability, and Evaluation

In the December 1999/January 2000 issue of *CMA Management Monthly,* the newsletter of the Christian Management Association, Mark Barrett, senior pastor at Ocean Hills Community Church in San Juan Capistrano, California, is quoted as having the following reminder posted in his office:

1. Healthy things grow.
2. Growing things change.
3. Changing things challenge us.
4. Challenge forces us to trust God.
5. Trust leads to obedience.
6. Obedience makes us healthy.
7. Healthy things grow.

I like that reminder and have shared it with many pastors and leaders in our healthy church training seminars. It's a wonderful summary of the key concepts required for us to grow in healthy ways. First of all, we are required to change. As a result of change, we are challenged to trust God and grow in our obedience to him. When we are open to change in light of our loving relationship with God, we become healthier in his sight. The health of the body of Christ in all its fullness requires simple obedience. Simple obedience leads to change. It's that cyclical pattern of growth that reminds us of the lifelong journey of faith on which each of us has embarked. Openness to his changes for us requires a spirituality that rises above our individual interests and embraces the needs of the whole body.

Inevitably, by the time you complete the exercises suggested in this workbook, you and your team will be confronted with the realities of change management, accountability, and evaluation. Since the goal of ministry is changed— transformed—lives, then you need to prayerfully consider the need for embracing the suggested exercises in this workbook. Change management, accountability, and evaluation are important for a variety of reasons, most specifically the following.

Regarding Change

One leader may say, "You mean to tell me that we need to introduce *changes* as a result of these exercises? No way!" while another will chime in, "Hallelujah, finally we will implement some long overdue *changes!* Praise God!" Others will be torn between both of these emotions and will watch on the sidelines before stepping forward to express their allegiances.

Since change is inevitable, what are leaders to do when it finally comes to this point? *Manage* the necessary changes so that the planning group and the congregation are enfolded into the process.

Learning how to anticipate change is the best place to begin! While I am not able to be exhaustive here, let me suggest a few pointers concerning the anticipation and management of change:

1. *Find your greatest—not least—common denominator in the decisions surrounding the proposed change and go for it!* Everyone won't be equally excited about the changes

being introduced. For the people pleaser, this truth is a difficult pill to swallow! The goal to strive for is unity, not unanimity!

2. *Communicate, communicate, communicate.* The greatest problems arise in seasons of change when the leader forgets to communicate, ineffectively communicates, or avoids communicating. The key questions to answer with clarity in all your communication surround the basic questions: Why? What? Who? When? Where? How?

3. *Appoint a person to spearhead the change(s) being introduced.* The management and monitoring of the implementation stages of each change is critical to the success of each one. Share the management of changes with members of the team, but be sure there is one person assigned to champion the process.

4. *Make sure that everyone involved in implementing the change(s) is clear on their assignments.* If it's foggy at the front end, it will unravel every step of the way. Be clear, concise, and provide all the necessary tools for each participant to successfully fulfill his or her assignment.

5. *Plan each stage of implementation in advance of execution.* Spell out the steps that will be necessary before beginning the process. Good planning results in well-orchestrated change.

6. *Celebrate the accomplishments of the group as the changes are being implemented successfully.* Don't wait until the end of the process to celebrate. Watch for milestones that can be highlighted and applauded all along the way. In the midst of your celebrations, savor the adventure and find joy in the change journey. This positive attitude toward change will help your team immeasurably.

7. *Be alert to innuendos and direct statements about the purpose(s) and/or selected methodologies of the change(s) being implemented, and directly speak to each issue raised.* Don't let questions and concerns be left unattended. Speak forthrightly to each person and/or group that raises issues and make sure that any misunderstandings are cleared up and not allowed to fester or become cancerous to the process.

8. *Acknowledge the potential grieving process of those affected by the change(s).* If you are shutting down an old program, recognize the value that program may have had in the lives of your congregants in the past. If you are introducing a new organization chart, remember that the old one once had meaning and significance to the previous generation, and members of that generation may still be in your church, or, at minimum, related to those in your church today. Don't mistreat those who may grieve in the midst of change. It's a very real emotion and should not be ignored or maligned.

9. *Encourage creativity from everyone involved in the change.* Your initial ideas may need to be altered or "tweaked" in order to be most effective. Even with the proposed change, there may need to be additional changes. Invite constructive, creative, and sometimes chaotic suggestions. Managing change is a dynamic process and should not be treated in a static manner. Learning how to adapt quickly to the changes coming your way will ease the resistances you may encounter.

10. *PRAY.* By far the most important piece of advice for you and your team is to pray. With open, outstretched hands, be prayerful in all aspects of the change process. Trust the Lord to guide your steps. Turn to him for direction and wisdom and strength. Transition from your present form of ministry to your future in the presence of the Holy One who longs to reveal his will to you and empower you for effective service. Changes are inevitable when we seek his face and invite him into the transformational process of growth and development for our local church and our personal lives. As you pray, thank him for the joy of serving him "for such a time as this."

We must be ready to meet the new changes, challenges, and needs of each generation. Be open to considering change(s) and find joy in the journey! The cost of mismanaging change is great. William Bridges, a well-known business consultant and preeminent authority on change and managing change, describes the real and measurable costs of not managing changes effectively as "GRASS: Guilt, Resentment, Anxiety, Self-absorption, and Stress." I couldn't agree more! Learning how to manage change is worth the effort—guaranteed.

Regarding Accountability

For many church leaders, the notion of accountability is a frightening concept to say the least! One leader may say, "I am accountable to God alone!" while from another you may hear, "I won't move ahead without your permission." The majority of leaders will stand somewhere in between these extremes. What is your notion of accountability and how is it lived out in your church?

I am a big believer in the need for accountability structures that empower people to become everything God intends. When systems of accountability curtail God's work in a person's life, then they are counterproductive for the individual and the kingdom of God. Finding a healthy balance between God-directed and human-trusted accountability is the goal.

Every person or group within the church needs to be held accountable. Each person serving in a ministry capacity needs someone or some group to turn to for support and accountability. Each group or committee needs to be accountable to the main board(s) of the church. Each staff person needs to be held accountable by the senior pastor. The senior pastor needs to be held accountable by the key lay leadership board (elders or deacons, depending on your structure). The key lay leaders are accountable to the wider congregation. The wider congregation is accountable to the denomination (or, in independent settings, to one another). No one is exempt from accountability. Therefore, when the subject is addressed, no one is left out!

For more than two decades, I have submitted myself to the disciplines of accountability that have dramatically influenced my daily life and ministry. By far one of the greatest tools for me has been weekly staff reports. Every Sunday night I complete these reports in my home as I reflect on my previous week and plan for the week ahead. I focus my attention prayerfully and reflectively on where the Lord led me in the past week and where I went in my own direction that proved to be counter to the Spirit's direction. I look ahead prayerfully to what's already on my schedule and reflect on what needs to be altered or changed in accordance to where I think the Lord would have me direct my energies. I share and discuss the essence of these reports with others—my wife, my accountability partner, and those in authority over me in my ministry.

Accountability is key to our growth—personally and collectively. If you are a leader in the church today, the value and priority of accountability structures needs to begin with you. As you experience their important place in your daily life, you will—by experience—introduce them into the life of the church.

Some of the ways that I see accountability being fulfilled in local churches include the following:

1. *SMART goals.* The place to begin every form of accountability is by knowing what the person or group is seeking to accomplish. Our goals become our benchmark for evaluation.
2. *Trusting relationships.* There is nothing worse than to be supervised by a person or group that you don't trust. Be sure that the quality of your relationships fosters healthy accountability. If the relational trust is not present, begin there before introducing accountability systems. Any system for maintaining a sense of accountable relationships flows first out of genuine, Christlike love. Empathetic, heartfelt love builds trust between people. In an atmosphere of trust we are willing to be vulnerable to one another.

If you are being supervised by someone you don't trust, ask the Lord if there are ways you can contribute to building that trust or to change the heart of your supervisor or ask the Lord to lead you into a new ministry under the care of a leader you can and do trust.

When the one you supervise knows with certainty that you have his or her best interests in mind, the ministry of accountability harvests great fruit for the kingdom!

3. *Weekly reports.* For the church staff, I encourage weekly accountability reports. They can be uniform in nature or individualized to the person but should include subjects like significant contacts, major accomplishments or highlights, key issues and concerns, plans for the upcoming week or month, personal growth and balance (i.e., relationship with God, reading list, diet, exercise, rest, fun, family, friendships, etc.).

For those individuals and groups that are not serving full time in ministry, *monthly reports* are the best option. Adjust expectations for part-time staff and volunteer teams while not losing the accountability report priority—the written reports have incredible value for all who serve as leaders in the congregation and need to be shared in appropriate settings (i.e., monthly board meetings).

4. *Ongoing communication.* Effective accountability structures include regular checks on progress, needs, concerns, refinements, redirections, and relationships. This communication needs to be prioritized in the schedules of each person involved, but should be initiated by the supervisor, while the information flow needs to be in both directions. Communication is the key ingredient to developing empathetic, effective, long-term relationships of accountability that work!

5. *Annual assessment.* Scheduling the annual evaluation is usually the biggest challenge here. Once scheduled, there are a variety of methods possible for achieving this goal. The Vision New England web site, www.VisionNewEngland.com, offers annual performance review forms for use with pastoral staff, ministry staff, administrators, and volunteers. Each group and key leaders should be assessed in their ministry assignment. Similar in purpose to the annual church health assessment, reviews for individuals on the team coalesce the

overall strategy of the church with each person serving in the various ministries. Uniting the overall vision and mission of the congregation with the key leaders' respective ministry is worth the effort. If performed with utmost seriousness, this process can produce great effectiveness in every aspect of your shared ministry for years to come.

Regarding Evaluation

If you hold to a view of ministry that values longevity, then you must be willing to hang in there through the multiple changes necessary to sustain the team and the ministry for the long haul. Ongoing evaluation is a required skill for today's long-term leaders. Learning how to ask the right questions about yourself, your team, and your shared ministry leads to greater effectiveness. Do you embrace the priority of this discipline? Frankly, it's a primary responsibility of leaders.

When you make a commitment to the ongoing evaluation and assessment process, you are making a commitment to leadership development—for you and your team. Each day you are making judgment calls on ministry effectiveness, whether purposefully or inadvertently. These judgment calls focus on areas of vision, mission, commitment, competencies, building community, and changing lives. The evaluation process is a link to greater health as a church as you continuously resharpen, refocus, and renew your structures and ministries.

Planning is a continual process, not a singular event. If you treat it as an event, it will produce what a stand-alone event will achieve. You want more than that. You want transformational ministry that makes a significant difference in the hearts and lives of every member of your congregation. That's why the dialogue, assessment, and planning process is the focus of this workbook. It takes considerable effort and discipline for leaders to pull this off, but the results are so strikingly obvious and distinctly different from those who do not exercise the dialogue, assessment, and planning options that they should propel every church leader to an ongoing commitment to this discipline. It's a doable process that virtually every church, no matter the size or current state of health, can accomplish.

It's time to embrace the process and dive in head first. The tools provided for you in this workbook will be helpful for you every step of the way. Don't be afraid of the process. Take it one step at a time, one big question at a time. Don't jump ahead of the process. Instead, allow the Holy Spirit to direct your every step and determine from the beginning to establish your leadership posture as a listener rather than an expert. You are all in this together as a leadership team and as a congregation. Each of you wants the same objective to be achieved—to become a healthy church. So be willing to count the cost and pay the price, because the end results will be for the glory of God.

I agree with Bill and Lynn Hybels, who counted the cost and paid a hefty price in leading the Willow Creek Community Church into greater and greater effectiveness over the past twenty-plus years. They understand the reason the process of planning is so important, especially if we are passionate about developing ministries that reflect the heart of God. They write in *Rediscovering Church* (Hybels and Hybels, Zondervan, 1995):

> You tell me: what is nobler, what is loftier, what is a higher purpose in life than devoting yourself to establishing and developing a community of believers that strives to fulfill the Acts 2 description of the bride of Christ? To creating a supportive and encouraging place where Spirit-led preaching brings a new, God-focused direction to people's lives; where believers gather in small groups to share their hearts on the deepest levels; where people compassionately walk with each other through life's problems and pain; where everyone feels empowered to make a difference through their spiritual gifts; where prayer, worship, and the sacraments are lifted up; where the rich share their God-given resources with the poor; and where people ache so much for their irreligious friends that the church gets strategic and takes risks to reach out to them with the Gospel?

page 163

The healthy church gets strategic and takes risks. The healthy church is God's church—fit for worship, relationships, and service that honors him and builds his kingdom! If changed lives are your bottom line in ministry, then take one step at a time as you think and act strategically—all for his glory and for the expansion of his kingdom!

God bless you every step of the way!

Ephesians 3: 14–21 was Paul's prayer for the Ephesian church and is my prayer for you:

> *For this reason I kneel before the Father, from whom his whole family in heaven and on earth derives its name. I pray that out of his glorious riches he may strengthen you with power through his Spirit in your inner being, so that Christ may dwell in your hearts through faith. And I pray that you, being rooted and established in love, may have power, together with all the saints, to grasp how wide and long and high and deep is the love of Christ, and to know this love that surpasses knowledge—that you may be filled to the measure of all the fullness of God.*
>
> *Now to him who is able to do immeasurably more than all we ask or imagine, according to his power that is at work within us, to him be glory in the church and in Christ Jesus throughout all generations, for ever and ever! Amen.*

Part 4

Additional Resources

Additional Scripture References for Each Characteristic

Characteristic 1: God's Empowering Presence

Holy Spirit

Romans 8:16 The Spirit himself testifies with our spirit that we are God's children.

1 Corinthians 12:7 To each one the manifestation of the Spirit is given . . .

Ephesians 4:3–6 Make every effort to keep the unity of the Spirit . . .

Fruit of the Spirit

Galatians 5:22–26 The fruit of the Spirit is love, joy, peace . . .

1 Timothy 1:16 I was shown mercy so that in me, the worst of sinners, Christ Jesus might display his unlimited patience . . .

1 Peter 4:10–11 Each one should use whatever gift he has received to serve others. . . . so that in all things God may be praised . . .

Spiritual Gifts:

1 Corinthians 12:1 Now about spiritual gifts, brothers, I do not want you to be ignorant.

Romans 12:4–8

1 Corinthians 12:1–30; 14:1–39

Ephesians 4:11–16

1 Peter 4:7–11

Characteristic 2: God-Exalting Worship

Worship

John 4:23 Yet a time is coming and has now come when the true worshipers will worship . . .

Romans 12:1 . . . offer your bodies as living sacrifices, holy and pleasing to God—this is your spiritual act of worship.

Holiness of God

Isaiah 6:1–4 I saw the Lord seated on a throne . . .

Cleansing, Empowerment, Service

Isaiah 6:5–8 . . . For I am a man of unclean lips. . . . Here I am. Send me!

Jeremiah 24:6–7 . . . I will build them up and not tear them down. . . . I will give them a heart to know me . . .

Zephaniah 3:17 . . . he will quiet you with his love, he will rejoice over you with singing.

Forms of Worship

Psalm 4:4 . . . search your hearts and be silent.

Psalm 95:6 Come, let us bow down in worship, let us kneel before the LORD our Maker.

Psalm 63:4 . . . and in your name I will lift up my hands.

Psalm 141:2 . . . may the lifting of my hands be like the evening sacrifice.

1 Timothy 2:8 I want men everywhere to lift up holy hands in prayer . . .

Psalm 47:1 Clap your hands, all you nations . . .

Psalm 33:2 Praise the LORD with the harp; make music to him on the ten-stringed lyre.

Psalm 92:3 . . . the music of the ten-stringed lyre and the melody of the harp.

Psalm 98:6 With trumpets and the blast of the ram's horn—shout for joy before the LORD, the King.

Psalm 144:9 . . . on the ten-stringed lyre I will make music to you . . .

Psalm 150:4 praise him with tambourine and dancing . . .

Genesis 24:26, 52 Then the man bowed down and worshiped the LORD. . . . When Abraham's servant heard what they said, he bowed down to the ground before the LORD.

Psalm 3:3 . . . you bestow glory on me and lift up my head.

Psalm 123:1 I lift up my eyes to you . . .

Psalm 32:11 Rejoice in the LORD and be glad, you righteous; sing, all you who are upright in heart!

Psalm 47:6 Sing praises to God, sing praises; sing praises to our King, sing praises.

Psalm 59:16 But I will sing of your strength, in the morning I will sing of your love . . .

Psalm 66:8 . . . let the sound of his praise be heard.

Psalm 69:30 I will praise God's name in song and glorify him with thanksgiving.

Psalm 98:1 Sing to the LORD a new song, for he has done marvelous things . . .

Psalm 100:1–2 Shout for joy to the LORD, all the earth. Worship the LORD with gladness; come before him with joyful songs.

Psalm 132:9 May your priests be clothed with righteousness; may your saints sing for joy.

Romans 1:9 God, whom I serve with my whole heart . . .

Romans 12:11–15 . . . keep your spiritual fervor, serving the Lord. Be joyful in hope, patient in affliction, faithful in prayer. . . .

Philippians 2:3–5 . . . Your attitude should be the same as that of Christ Jesus . . . taking the very nature of a servant, being made in human likeness.

1 Timothy 4:7–8 . . . train yourself to be godly. . . . godliness has value for all things, holding promise for both the present life and the life to come.

Characteristic 3: Spiritual Disciplines

1 Kings 19:9–13 . . . the LORD was not in the wind. . . . the LORD was not in the earthquake. . . . the LORD was not in the fire. And after the fire came a gentle whisper . . .

Psalm 25:4–5 Show me your ways, O LORD . . .

Psalm 46:10 Be still, and know that I am God . . .

Psalm 62:5 Find rest, O my soul, in God alone . . .

Isaiah 61:3 They will be called oaks of righteousness, a planting of the LORD for the display of his splendor.

Jeremiah 33:3 Call to me and I will answer you . . .

Matthew 22:34–40 Love the Lord your God with all your heart . . .

Matthew 25:35–36 For I was hungry and you gave me something to eat . . .

Luke 10:38–42 . . . you are worried and upset about many things, but only one thing is needed. Mary has chosen what is better . . .

John 6:25–40 . . . Do not work for food that spoils, but for food that endures to eternal life, which the Son of Man will give you. . . .

James 3:17 But the wisdom that comes from heaven is first of all pure . . .

Characteristic 4: Learning and Growing in Community

Luke 9:14 Have them sit down in groups of about fifty each.

Romans 14:19 Let us therefore make every effort to do what leads to peace . . .

James 5:16 Therefore confess your sins to each other and pray for each other . . .

Love One Another

John 13:34–35 A new command I give you: Love one another. As I have loved you . . .

Romans 13:8 Let no debt remain outstanding, except the continuing debt to love one another . . .

1 Corinthians 12:24–25 . . . there should be no division in the body, but that its parts should have equal concern for each other.

1 Peter 1:22 Now that you have purified yourselves by obeying the truth so that you have sincere love for your brothers, love one another deeply from the heart.

1 Peter 5:14 Greet one another with a kiss of love. . . .

1 John 3:11 This is the message you heard from the beginning: We should love one another.

Encourage and Build Each Other Up

Galatians 6:2 Carry each other's burdens, and in this way you will fulfill the law of Christ.

1 Thessalonians 5:11 Therefore encourage one another and build each other up . . .

Hebrews 3:13 But encourage one another daily . . . so that none of you may be hardened by sin's deceitfulness.

Hebrews 10:25 Let us not give up meeting together . . . but let us encourage one another . . .

Submit and Admonish

Ephesians 4:2 Be completely humble and gentle; be patient, bearing with one another in love.

Ephesians 5:21 Submit to one another out of reverence for Christ.

Colossians 3:13 Bear with each other and forgive whatever grievances you may have against one another. Forgive as the Lord forgave you.

Colossians 3:16 Let the word of Christ dwell in you richly as you teach and admonish one another . . .

Serve

Matthew 10:24–25 A student is not above his teacher . . .

Galatians 5:13 . . . do not use your freedom to indulge the sinful nature; rather, serve one another in love.

Hebrews 10:24 And let us consider how we may spur one another on toward love and good deeds.

Characteristic 5: A Commitment to Loving and Caring Relationships

1 John 3:11, 16–18 . . . This is how we know what love is: Jesus Christ laid down his life for us. And we ought to lay down our lives for our brothers.

The Beatitudes

Matthew 5:3–10 Blessed are the poor in spirit . . . Blessed are those who hunger and thirst for righteousness . . .

Grace, Mercy, Forgiveness

Psalm 51 Have mercy on me, O God, according to your unfailing love . . .

Psalm 85:10 Love and faithfulness meet together; righteousness and peace kiss each other.

Psalm 103:17 But from everlasting to everlasting the Lord's love is with those who fear him, and his righteousness with their children's children.

Psalm 108:4 For great is your love, higher than the heavens; your faithfulness reaches to the skies.

Lamentations 3:22–23 Because of the Lord's great love we are not consumed, for his compassions never fail. They are new every morning . . .

Micah 6:8 He has showed you, O man, what is good. . . .

Micah 7:18 Who is a God like you, who pardons sin and forgives the transgression . . .

Matthew 5:7 Blessed are the merciful, for they will be shown mercy.

Matthew 9:13 . . . I desire mercy, not sacrifice. For I have not come to call the righteous, but sinners.

Matthew 18:23–35 Therefore, the kingdom of heaven is like a king who wanted to settle accounts with his servants. . . .

Matthew 25:34–36 . . . For I was hungry and you gave me . . .

Luke 10:30–37 . . . A man was going down from Jerusalem to Jericho, when he fell into the hands of robbers. . . . Which of these three do you think was a neighbor to the man who fell into the hands of robbers?

Luke 15:11–32 . . . because this brother of yours was dead and is alive again; he was lost and is found.

2 Timothy 1:16–18 May the Lord show mercy to the household of Onesiphorus, because he often refreshed me and was not ashamed of my chains. . . .

God's Commandments

Exodus 20:1–17 . . . I am the LORD your God . . .

Matthew 22:37–40 . . . Love the Lord your God with all your heart and with all your soul and with all your mind. . . .

The Great Commission

Matthew 28:18–20 . . . Therefore go and make disciples of all nations . . .

Compassionate, Not Judgmental

Matthew 7:1–5 Do not judge, or you too will be judged. . . .

Matthew 9:36 When he saw the crowds, he had compassion on them . . .

Matthew 10:29–31 Are not two sparrows sold for a penny? Yet not one of them will fall . . .

Matthew 15:29–39 . . . He told the crowd to sit down on the ground. Then he took the seven loaves and the fish . . .

Luke 6:37–38 Do not judge, and you will not be judged. Do not condemn . . .

John 8:7 . . . If any one of you is without sin, let him be the first to throw a stone at her.

James 2:12–13 Speak and act as those who are going to be judged by the law . . .

Resolving Conflict

Genesis 4 . . . Then the LORD said to Cain, "Why are you angry? . . . If you do what is right, will you not be accepted? . . ."

Genesis 37 . . . When his brothers saw that their father loved him more than any of them, they hated him and could not speak a kind word to him. . . .

Acts 6:1–6 . . . Brothers, choose seven men from among you who are known to be full of the Spirit and wisdom. . . .

Acts 15:36–40 . . . They had such a sharp disagreement that they parted company. . . .

Romans 12:9–18 . . . Honor one another above yourselves. . . .

1 Corinthians 14:4–8 He who speaks in a tongue edifies himself, but he who prophesies edifies the church. . . .

James 3:13–18 Who is wise and understanding among you? . . . But the wisdom that comes from heaven is . . . peace-loving . . .

1 Peter 4:12 Dear friends, do not be surprised at the painful trial you are suffering . . .

Holy Living

Matthew 6:33 But seek first his kingdom and his righteousness . . .

2 Corinthians 5:16–21 . . . the old has gone, the new has come! All this is from God, who reconciled us to himself through Christ and gave us the ministry of reconciliation . . .

Ephesians 4:22–32 You were taught, with regard to your former way of life, to put off your old self . . .

Colossians 3:12–17 . . . clothe yourselves with compassion, kindness, humility . . . Bear with each other and forgive . . .

1 Timothy 2:1–8 I urge, then, first of all, that requests, prayers, intercession and thanksgiving be made for everyone . . .

Hebrews 12:1–3 Therefore, since we are surrounded by such a great cloud of witnesses . . .

Characteristic 6: Servant-Leadership Development

Mark 10:42–45 . . . whoever wants to be first must be slave of all. . . .

John 10:14–15 I am the good shepherd; I know my sheep . . .

John 13:1–17 . . . he now showed them the full extent of his love. . . .

John 21:18 . . . someone else will dress you and lead you . . .

Ephesians 4:11–13 . . . some to be apostles, some to be prophets . . . so that the body of Christ may be built up until we all reach unity in the faith . . .

Ephesians 4:16 From him the whole body, joined and held together . . .

Philippians 2:3–8 Do nothing out of selfish ambition . . .

1 Thessalonians 2:6–12 . . . For you know that we dealt with each of you as a father deals with his own children . . .

2 Timothy 2:2 And the things you have heard me say in the presence of many witnesses entrust to reliable men who will also be qualified to teach others.

1 Peter 5:2–4 . . . serving as overseers—not because you must, but because you are willing . . . eager to serve . . .

Characteristic 7: An Outward Focus

Psalm 34:8 Taste and see that the LORD is good . . .

Matthew 10:40 He who receives you receives me, and he who receives me receives the one who sent me.

John 17:23 . . . May they be brought to complete unity . . .

Luke 19:10 For the Son of Man came to seek and to save what was lost.

Luke 10:25–28 . . . Love the Lord your God with all your heart and with all your soul . . . and, Love your neighbor as yourself.

1 Thessalonians 1:5 . . . our gospel came to you not simply with words, but also with power . . .

Suffering for His Name

Acts 5:41 The apostles left the Sanhedrin, rejoicing because they had been counted worthy of suffering disgrace for the Name.

Romans 5:3 . . . because we know that suffering produces perseverance; perseverance, character . . .

2 Timothy 1:8 So do not be ashamed to testify about our Lord, or be ashamed of me his prisoner. But join with me in suffering for the gospel . . .

Hebrews 2:10 . . . it was fitting that God . . . should make the author of their salvation perfect through suffering.

1 Peter 3:17 It is better, if it is God's will, to suffer for doing good than for doing evil.

Bearing Fruit

John 15 *The vine and the branches*

Being a Witness

2 Chronicles 7:14 If my people . . . will humble themselves and pray and seek my face . . .

Isaiah 63:7 I will tell of the kindnesses of the LORD . . .

Jeremiah 20:9 . . . his word is in my heart like a fire . . .

Matthew 28:18–20 . . . Therefore go and make disciples of all nations . . .

Acts 1:8 But you will receive power when the Holy Spirit comes on you; and you will be my witnesses . . .

Acts 2:47 . . . those who were being saved.

Acts 5:20–21 . . . tell the people the full message of this new life. . . .

Acts 22:14–15 . . . You will be his witness to all men of what you have seen and heard.

Romans 10:14–15 . . . How beautiful are the feet of those who bring good news!

Romans 10:17 . . . faith comes from hearing the message, and the message is heard through the word of Christ.

Ephesians 6:19 Pray also for me, that whenever I open my mouth, words may be given me so that I will fearlessly make known the mystery of the gospel.

1 Thessalonians 2 . . . We loved you so much that we were delighted to share with you not only the gospel of God but our lives as well . . .

1 Peter 3:15 . . . Always be prepared to give an answer . . .

Characteristic 8: Wise Administration and Accountability

Exodus 30–40 *God's plan for ministry given to Moses*

Nehemiah 1–13 *Nehemiah's wise administration*

1 Chronicles 28–29 *David's plan for the temple*

Proverbs 3:5–8 . . . and lean not on your own understanding . . .

Jeremiah 18:3–6 . . . so the potter formed it into another pot . . .

Luke 16:11 . . . who will trust you with true riches?

Characteristic 9: Networking with the Body of Christ

Psalm 133:1 . . . when brothers live together in unity!

John 10:30 I and the Father are one.

John 17:11 . . . so that they may be one as we are one.

John 17:21 . . . that all of them may be one, Father, just as you are in me and I am in you.

John 17:23 I in them and you in me. May they be brought to complete unity to let the world know . . .

1 Corinthians 6:17 But he who unites himself with the Lord is one with him in spirit.

1 Corinthians 12:9–11 . . . All these [spiritual gifts] are the work of one and the same Spirit. . . .

1 Corinthians 12:12 The body is a unit, though it is made up of many parts; and though all its parts are many, they form one body. So it is with Christ.

1 Corinthians 12:14–20 . . . If the whole body were an eye, where would the sense of hearing be? . . . there are many parts, but one body.

1 Corinthians 12:27 Now you are the body of Christ . . .

Galatians 3:28 There is neither Jew nor Greek . . . for you are all one in Christ Jesus.

Ephesians 2:18 For through him we both have access to the Father by one Spirit.

Ephesians 3:14–21 . . . And I pray that you, being rooted and established in love, may have power, together with all the saints . . .

Ephesians 4:4 There is one body and one Spirit . . .

Colossians 3:15 Let the peace of Christ rule in your hearts . . .

1 Timothy 2:5 For there is one God and one mediator between God and men, the man Christ Jesus.

Hebrews 2:11 Both the one who makes men holy and those who are made holy are of the same family. . . .

Characteristic 10: Stewardship and Generosity

Matthew 6:21 For where your treasure is, there your heart will be also.

Matthew 21:33–46 There was a landowner who planted a vineyard. . . .

Matthew 24–25 *Other kingdom teachings and parables*

Matthew 25:14–30 Again, it will be like a man going on a journey, who called his servants and entrusted his property to them. . . . "Well done, good and faithful servant!"

Mark 13:32–37 No one knows about that day or hour. . . . Be on guard! Be alert! . . .

Luke 12:32 . . . your Father has been pleased to give you the kingdom.

Luke 13:28 . . . when you see Abraham, Isaac and Jacob and all the prophets in the kingdom of God . . .

Luke 17:21 . . . the kingdom of God is within you.

Luke 19:11–27 . . . A man of noble birth went to a distant country. . . . So he called ten of his servants and gave them ten minas. . . .

2 Corinthians 8:1–15 . . . they gave as much as they were able, and even beyond their ability. . . .

2 Corinthians 9:6 Whoever sows sparingly will also reap sparingly . . .

Sermon Outlines for Each Characteristic

by David Midwood
Vice President of Church Leadership Services
Vision New England

Characteristic 1: God's Empowering Presence

The healthy church actively seeks the Holy Spirit's direction and empowerment for its daily life and ministry.

Sermon Text: Acts 2:1–4

When the day of Pentecost came, they were all together in one place. Suddenly a sound like the blowing of violent wind came from heaven and filled the whole house where they were sitting. They saw what seemed to be tongues of fire that separated and came to rest on each of them. All of them were filled with the Holy Spirit and began to speak in other tongues as the Spirit enabled them.

The first of the characteristics of the healthy church is that it actively seeks the Holy Spirit's direction and empowerment for its daily life and ministry. The absolute necessity of the Holy Spirit's power and presence is clearly demonstrated when the Day of Pentecost came to the 120 assembled believers, all people of prayer and faith. All of those who were gathered had experienced the powerful ministry of Jesus Christ. The disciples were there, the seventy, who had already been sent out by the Savior to perform miraculous signs and wonders. Others joined them who had endured persecution and trouble to walk with Jesus Christ. Yet all of them without exception needed the power of the Holy Spirit. The Savior had instructed them not to leave Jerusalem until they had experienced God's empowering presence.

There can be no substitute for this first characteristic of a healthy church. Neither organization nor legalism nor pleasing personalities nor powerful enthusiasm can substitute for the empowering presence of God's Holy Spirit.

I. The Holy Spirit came at Pentecost (v. 1)
  A. This was God's chosen and appointed time
    1. God is pleased to send refreshment at specific times and seasons in the life of his church. In New England God has taught this lesson to those who live along the coastline and have experienced the changing and cleansing tides. He has also taught this same lesson in the changing seasons of the year: winter, spring, summer, and fall.
    2. Jesus said, "the wind blows where it will." In this he taught that the work of God by the Holy Spirit is sovereign. In the individual, the local church, the region, and the nation, God sends his

Spirit and his Word to accomplish his purpose according to his omnipotent design.

B. Pentecost is God's harvest festival time
In Israel, when the Day of Pentecost came, evidence of the harvest was waved before God in worship as a consecration of the entire harvest in thanksgiving to God. The significance of Pentecost is the arrival of the time to gather in the harvest.

1. It was a strategic time. Crowds from every region gathered in Jerusalem. Ethnic diversity is represented, as the whole catalogue of languages is later documented in this chapter. An international harvest began on the Day of Pentecost.

2. "They were all together in one place." When Christians are gathered in unity, God is pleased to pour out his Holy Spirit. These believers were gathered in unity in prayer and relationship. God does not pour out his Holy Spirit on contentious people. Unhappy divisions stifle our usefulness to God. Pride, prejudice, and apathy hinder our reception of God's empowering presence. The church that is unified in its desire for Christ and his kingdom without contention is a place where God will work.

II. When the Spirit comes with power
A. "Suddenly" (v. 2)
When people are going to accomplish something it requires great planning, great organization, great equipment, and lots of manpower. When God is going to accomplish something he does it "suddenly."

B. "A sound" (v. 2)
The Spirit of God is silent yet the impact of his work is not silent. The results of the Spirit's presence were heard on this day and will be heard throughout the world. The sound of a violent wind meant that the voice of God's people would be heard throughout the world.

C. "Wind" (v. 2)

In both the Old Testament and the New Testament the word for *wind* and *spirit* is the same. Jesus compares wind and spirit in John 3:8. He says that the wind is mysterious, comes and goes as it will. We are reminded here that our God is not tame, predictable, or boring. He is the awesome, omnipotent God of the Bible. This wind of the Spirit will move this gathering of 120 believers into the whole world. But without God's empowering presence, we creep, crawl, and measure our gains by inches. The text describes the wind as "blowing" and "violent." A wind, which nothing could withstand, shook the entire place where the believers were gathered, reminding us that there is nothing that can stop the Spirit's progress.

D. "Filled the whole house where they were sitting" (v. 2)
God is not confined to one place, one room, one sanctuary, or one church. When his empowering presence comes, he fills the entire place with his presence.

E. "Tongues of fire" (v. 3)
God, who is a consuming fire, reveals himself here. He was like a pillar of fire in the wilderness journey of his people, and now on the Day of Pentecost this same God of fire hovers over the New Testament church. It is the same fire for all believers, but the fire appears individually over each Christian.

F. "Came to rest on each of them" (v. 3)
This indicates the abiding influence of the Holy Spirit as he works through each individual's unique character and personality.

III. The infilling of God's empowering presence
A. "All of them were filled with the Holy Spirit" (v. 4)
The sounds of the Spirit's presence and the tongues of fire were symbols of the Spirit's presence. The real work is now accomplished as believers are filled with the Holy Spirit.

1. God's empowering presence is not a divisive factor in the church but rather

a unifying factor. *All* of the believers are filled with the Spirit. This is not some optional, extracurricular, special endowment given to some. Jesus teaches in John 3:5–6 that flesh gives birth to flesh but the Spirit gives birth to spirit.

2. The apostle Paul exhorts all believers in Ephesians 5:18 to continue being filled with the Spirit. The fullness of the Spirit, as the apostle Paul teaches, is not measured in quarts or gallons but is manifest in singing "psalms, hymns and spiritual songs. . . . in your heart to the Lord, always giving thanks to God" (vv. 19–20). And the work of the Spirit is then seen in right relationship in marriage, family, and work. And in the powerful presence of God's kingdom in the face of spiritual warfare. The Bible gives a number of expressions of the fullness of the Spirit: peace in the midst of tumult, passion for truth, compassion for people, Christian growth, the fruit of the Spirit, and the gifts of the Spirit in action.

B. Peter, a case study

Peter, without God's empowering presence, brags to the Savior, "I'll never deny you." And yet soon he is cursing and swearing in denial of his savior Jesus Christ. Peter without the power of the Spirit sinks in the sea of unbelief and even dares to correct the Lord on several occasions.

1. Now we see Peter empowered by God's presence standing fearlessly in the midst of thousands of people. He powerfully declares that Jesus Christ is Lord, and three thousand people are converted.

2. Peter continues to be empowered by God's presence, healing people and declaring boldly before the rulers of his people, "We cannot help speaking about what we have seen and heard" (Acts 4:20).

3. We too will receive God's empowering presence as we are willing to yield more and more to the control of the Holy Spirit and experience the same powerful transformation that changed Peter.

IV. The impact of God's empowering presence

A. A sermon (vv. 14–36)

God gave his Spirit to help Peter preach. His sermon was effective because of its simplicity and clarity. Peter clearly preached the lordship of Jesus Christ. The fullness of the Spirit will make us preach Christ everywhere, simply, clearly, directly.

B. Conversions (vv. 37–41)

People called out after the sermon, "What do we have to do to be saved?" When our lives preach Jesus Christ, people will be drawn to him. This is the testimony of the onlookers in verse 11: "We hear them declaring the wonders of God in our own tongues!"

C. Outward confession (v. 41)

God's empowering presence now enables the converted to make an outward confession of the inner work of God's grace and transformation. They boldly declare their determination to follow Jesus Christ. This is the work of the Holy Spirit, which is absolutely essential when lost people come home to the love of God the Father.

Characteristic 2: God-Exalting Worship

The healthy church gathers regularly as the local expression of the body of Christ to worship God in ways that engage the heart, mind, soul, and strength of the people.

Sermon Text: Psalm 27:4

One thing I ask of the LORD, this is what I seek: that I may dwell in the house of the LORD all the days of my life, to gaze upon the beauty of the LORD and to seek him in his temple.

The Book of Psalms is the personal story of God-exalting worship. It is the story of God's people in prayer and praise. The revelations of truth are expressed in a variety of human experiences. The truth explodes with fire, passion, and emotions. Sometimes the writers are up and sometimes the writers are down, but the Psalms are stories of real people with real joy and real sorrow. We are privileged to listen as they open their hearts in God-exalting worship, bear their souls, and tell the truth about their struggles. Four dimensions of God-exalting worship emerge in the pages of the Psalms.

I. First, God-exalting worship is a lifestyle.

   A. In the blessed lift described in Psalm 1 the person who is godly meditates on the word of God day and night. In other psalms the writer talks about praising God morning, noon, and night or seven times a day.

   B. God-exalting worship is not reserved for one hour on Sunday morning. The apostle Paul appeals to us in Romans 12:1 "Therefore, I urge you, brothers, in view of God's mercy, to offer your bodies as living sacrifices, holy and pleasing to God—this is your spiritual act of worship."

   C. God-exalting worship is a way of life in which we offer ourselves as living sacrifices. As someone has pointed out, the problem with living sacrifices is that we keep crawling off the altar. A life of worship is what God has invited us to celebrate!

II. The second dimension of God-exalting worship is the bold passion for God alone.

   A. David seems to be well aware of what his life is all about. In the film *City Slickers* several men in midlife crisis are seeking to find out what life is all about as they visit a dude ranch and participate in a cattle drive. One of the characters inquires of a cowboy about the secret mystery of life. The cowboy responds that the mystery of life is in knowing what is your "one thing." In the psalms it is clear that David knows his "one thing" and that his passion is to dwell in the house of the Lord and behold God's beauty forever.

   B. A businessman trying to sort out his career and future direction was discussing his options with a highly paid consultant. After listening for a period of time the consultant drew a box and invited the businessman to write in the box his main objective in life. The consultant said he could help him and give him direction but he couldn't do anything until the businessman identified his main objective in life.

   C. David understood that he would find true satisfaction only in wholehearted worship. In 2 Samuel 13:14 David is described as "a man after God's own heart." He was an individual with total focus, deep commitment, and uncompromised devotion. It seems that God-exalting worship exploded in David's life on that day that he publicly led the celebration of God's people. "David . . . danced before the LORD with all his might" (2 Sam. 6:14). When his unenthusiastic wife tried to shame him, he responded by announcing, "I will become even more undignified than this, and I will be humiliated in my own eyes" (2 Sam. 6:22). This is worship with bold passion, worship that engages the entire person in loving God with all your heart, all your soul, and all your mind (Matt. 22:37).

III. The third dimension of God-exalting worship is worship that is a witness to the watching world.

   A. When someone is engaged in God-exalting worship and when the church is alive with God-exalting worship, the world around takes notice. David is confident of this when he says, "I will praise you, O LORD, among the nations; I sing of you among the peoples" (Ps. 57:9).

   B. David believed that God would bring unbelievers to himself through authentic worship. His own story is this, "He put a new song in my mouth, a hymn of praise to our God. Many will see and fear and put their trust in the LORD" (Ps. 40:3).

C. In the movie *Sister Act* Whoopee Goldberg, who had been a night club singer, is placed in a witness protection program and hidden away in a convent. Her musical and entertainment gifts are discovered and she transforms the tired, dreary choir into a power-packed explosion of dramatic praise. The individual choir members are transformed. The choir is energized. The church discovers new life and the entire community is changed. Hollywood has given us a refreshing illustration of the power of worship as a witness to the watching world.

IV. The fourth dimension of God-exalting worship is that of brokenness.

A. The psalms tell the stories of our authentic pain and suffering. Lives are shattered by betrayal, death, loss, and failure. The psalmist knows how to "sing the blues" in God-exalting worship.

B. The psalmist cries out in Psalm 51 for a clean heart.

C. Assurance is given that God is close to the brokenhearted in Psalm 34:18. And Psalm 147:3 asserts: "He heals the brokenhearted and binds up their wounds."

D. A few years ago a close friend was engaged in a life-and-death struggle with cancer. When he began chemotherapy treatments and his hair was falling out, a group of his friends gathered at the local barbershop to shave their heads in solidarity with him. They were all brokenhearted as their friend faced this battle of a lifetime.

During the time when one of the men had exceedingly short hair, he preached at a church in Rhode Island. On a subsequent visit to the church a man approached him and told him his story. His daughter had been battling a rare form of cancer. He had been attending church but couldn't seem to connect with God. When he heard the sermon

and why the preacher had shaved his head, there was a message for him not to give up, there was still hope for his situation. He made a decision to trust God. For him, it wasn't the sermon but it was a shaved head that showed him the love of God in a time of extreme brokenness.

V. Conclusion: A life enriched by God-exalting worship includes
A. A lifestyle of worship—morning, noon, and night
B. A bold passion for God alone
C. A witness to the watching world
D. A heart that is broken before God and yet filled with joy and hope

Characteristic 3: Spiritual Disciplines

The healthy church provides training, models, and resources for members of all ages to develop our daily spiritual disciplines.

Sermon Text: Psalm 1

Imagine for a moment that two friends planted gardens. They both prepared the ground and they both planted seeds, but after that everything changed. Mr. Lazy neglected his garden and simply waited for the vegetables to grow. But Mr. Faithful worked in his garden daily. He watered the garden, weeded the garden, put sticks around for growing tomato plants and cages around the young plants that the animals might disturb.

At harvesttime Mr. Lazy found rotting vegetables, wilting plants, and lots of weeds. The plants had fallen over because no support had been provided to keep them off the ground. The animals had also done their damage. Mr. Lazy's quick assessment was that gardens were just a waste of time. He could get better vegetables at the supermarket. He looked at Mr. Faithful's garden and grumbled to himself, "It seems that some people just have all the luck."

Mr. Faithful was harvesting beautiful vegetables almost every day. They tasted better than anything you could buy at the grocery store. He enjoyed an abundant harvest and especially enjoyed sharing his vegetables with his friends and neighbors. The harvest season for Mr. Faithful was his favorite season of the year.

Participation in the spiritual disciplines of the Christian life is a characteristic of healthy Christians, and healthy Christians are at the center of the work in a healthy church. The classic understanding of Christian maturity is that the inner life is like a garden that needs to be tended.

Psalm 1 is a summary of all that the Bible has to say about growing in godliness and godly living. If the Psalm had a title it might be called "The Two Ways." Verses 1–3 describe the way of life. Verses 4–5 describe the way of destruction. Verse 6 describes the final parting of the ways.

I. The way of life
This is the description of the godly man.
A. A life of blessedness
1. *Blessed* is a word that is often misused today. A sportscaster might announce that the New England Patriots are blessed to have a good linebacker.
2. *Blessed* in the Bible means having total fulfillment, deep satisfaction that comes from being in God's presence. This is the meaning of the Aaronic blessing:

> The LORD bless you and keep you;
> the LORD make his face shine upon you and be gracious to you;
> the LORD turn his face toward you and give you peace.
>
> Numbers 6:24–26

3. To be *blessed* is to be complete, to have your needs met, overflowing with love and the fullness of God's presence.
B. Input and output
The godly man is described in Psalm 1 in two ways. Verses 1–2 describe the inflow and input in his life. Verse 3 describes the outflow and output.
1. Input
a. His company (v. 1)
The godly person is known by the company he or she keeps. The godly individual is not influenced by the crowd of unbelievers. Four postures are used to describe the lifestyle of the godly individual.
(1) He does not walk in the counsel of the wicked, nor does he take their advice or live by their principles.
(2) He does not stand in the way of sinners by adopting their behavior or conforming to their ways.
(3) He does not sit in the seat of the scornful, taking up residence with those who scoff and ridicule with cynicism the way of the righteous.
(4) He is in fellowship with those who are godly. It is their advice, their ways, and their attitudes that help him live a godly lifestyle.
b. His meditation (v. 2)
(1) He delights in the instruction of God. The believer is always eager and longing to learn the Word and walk in obedience.
(2) He meditates, not just reads, but thinks about the Word, applies it to his life, personalizes it both day and night.
(3) The result is a lifestyle of relationship with God and a transformed life.
2. Output
a. The godly believer is productive (v. 3).
b. His character is stable. He is like a healthy tree. There is no drought in his spiritual life.
c. Believers bear fruit. This fruit contains the seed for new trees. Godly individuals reproduce themselves. Godly believers influence the life and growth of other godly believers.
d. In all he does he prospers.
II. The way of destruction
The wicked are not like the believers.
A. The great contrast
The intake and the output of believers is completely different from that of unbe-

lievers, who are compared to chaff. The chaff is the husk of the grain that is separated in the threshing process and thrown away. The wind blows the chaff away because it has no weight, no stability, and no use.

  B. The great divide

When the threshing is complete, unbelievers will be seen as useless. They're not stable like trees. They do not bear fruit.

III. The parting of the ways

  A. *Therefore* in verse 5 indicates a cause-and-effect relationship.

  B. An individual's lifestyle is called "a way" because no one stands still. Every action identifies you with the righteous or the unrighteous, believers or unbelievers. Our actions affect our character and our character determines our destiny.

  C. The writer has contrasted the actions of the godly and the ungodly. The writer has contrasted the character of the godly and the ungodly. And now the writer contrasts the destinies of the godly and the ungodly as they are revealed.

IV. The way of the wicked will perish

When a car is "totaled" it does not mean that the car ceases to exist. It means the car is incapable of doing anything that makes a car a car. In this sense to be cut off from God forever is to be "totaled," incapable of joy or love or doing anything that makes human existence meaningful.

 V. Conclusion

This Psalm, like Jesus' teaching about the two roads, one that leads to life and one that leads to destruction, teaches that no one is standing still but everyone is moving down one road or the other.

The believer is identified as an authentic individual by his pursuit of God. His delight is in the Law of God and his meditation is on the Law both day and night.

Only one man has achieved the full blessing of this Psalm. He is the ever blessed God-Man, Jesus Christ. It was always his delight to do the will of the Father. Yet for us he was willing to take the destiny of destruction and go to the cross so that he might offer himself to us who deserved destruction as the everlasting way of life. He is the One who meets us at these crossroads where the way of life and the way of doom and destruction lead in opposite directions. And he challenges us to examine our lives and choose wisely the path that we will travel.

Characteristic 4: Learning and Growing in Community

The healthy church encourages believers to grow in their walk with God and with one another in the context of a safe, affirming environment.

Sermon Text: Acts 2:42–47

Routine checkups are part of daily life. Physical checkups at the doctor's office include measuring blood pressure and weight and routine blood work. Checkups on our car involve routine maintenance and annual inspections. Financial checkups include analyses of income and investments and a review of our debt situation.

A church that is learning and growing in community is also identified by specific characteristics. These six verses in Acts 2:42–47 provide a profound insight into the life and community of early Christian believers.

I. The church learns together

"They devoted themselves to the apostles' teaching" (v. 42).

  A. "The apostles' teaching"

    1. Apostolic teaching was always intended to result in life transformation. A church that is proud of Bible preaching but full of bitterness, anger, and pride is unbalanced. A Bible teaching church should also be a Bible learning church where the things that are taught are also put into practice in the lives of believers.

    2. One of the amazing realities of the early Christians is the fact that they were just folks—fishermen, common people. But their lives had been trans-

formed through an encounter with Jesus Christ.

3. The early Christians were hungry for God's truth. They were unstoppable and not embarrassed to learn more and more through the apostles' teaching. Believers should never be afraid to attend Bible study or Christian education classes because they don't know very much about the Bible. If you can't learn in our classes, then we are doing something wrong.

B. "They devoted themselves"

1. *Devoted* means disciplined, consistent commitment.

2. Could anyone describe us as "devoted" to the study of the Scriptures and the commitment to live them out in daily life?

3. God has designed our life together to be a community where his Word can be rooted and grounded in our lives. This happens as we are learning together.

4. It is wise to think of the quest for truth like a search for gold. You must take the initiative in going after it, doing the hard work, digging, and searching. Biblical truth requires a search as we read, study, meditate, think, and listen.

5. A learning community is devoted to the truth and transformed by the truth.

II. The church fellowships and worships together

A. Fellowship, breaking bread, prayer (vv. 42, 46)

These activities took place in large groups at the temple and in small groups when they broke bread in their homes and when they ate together.

B. Sharing all things

1. This church had learned to share all things. To share their troubles as well as their joys, their breakthroughs as well as their burdens.

2. Christians are held together by the Holy Spirit in the same way that the

various parts of the body work together physically.

C. The mark of love

1. Jesus tells the disciples that it is their love that will be the authentic mark by which the world will know that they are truly his disciples (John 13:35). The authentic mark of true relationship with God is seen by the watching world in the way Christians express their love for each other.

2. The Savior's emphasis on the relational transformation brought by the gospel is simply essential in his design of his church.

3. To be a Bible believing church full of bad relationships is a contradiction of the Savior's clear command.

4. We are judged by our relationships whether we like it or not. Jesus said that Christians should treat each other in the way that they would like to be treated.

5. We are now empowered to love each other because we have first been loved by God.

III. The church is marked by generosity

"All the believers were together and had everything in common. Selling their possessions and goods they gave to anyone as he had need" (v. 44).

A. All belongs to God

All your resources belong to God. All your wealth belongs to God.

B. Reflecting God's character

There's something wrong with your understanding of Scripture and your Christian experience if you do not display generosity in your daily lifestyle. Cheap, stingy Christians do not reflect the generous character and nature of their heavenly Father.

C. Giving

Christian living and Christian giving go hand in hand. Authentic generosity always identifies true believers. Your giving gives you away!

IV. The church reaches the lost and adds to its community

"And the Lord added to their number daily those who were being saved" (v. 47).

A. Evangelism is a by-product of authentic Christian living

B. Real Christianity is contagious
It is not a gimmick that entices unbelievers into the church. The church has embarrassed itself too many times with schemes, programs, and plans that have been substituted for the authentic witness of Christians daily living out the gospel.

C. Real Christianity is noticed
"Everyone was filled with awe, and many wonders and miraculous signs were done by the apostles" (v. 43). These Christians in this church loved the Lord, loved the truth, loved each other, and loved to give generously. The watching world experienced the explosive impact of real Christianity in people who are simply described in verse 46 as people who had "glad and sincere hearts."

D. The outflow of normal Christian living
"The Lord added to their number" (v. 47). Day by day lost people were discovering true Christianity. This is the kind of church God is determined to bless.

Characteristic 5: A Commitment to Loving and Caring Relationships

The healthy church is intentional in its efforts to build loving, caring relationships within families, between members, and within the community we serve.

Sermon Title: Jesus Christ, Lord of Our Relationships

Sermon Text: Philippians 2:1–8

I. The model for our relationships: The Godhead (vv. 6–8)
A. Unity (John 17:20–21)
1. From the beginning of time and before time the Father, Son, and Holy Spirit have had a perfect personal relationship of love and communication.
What God has been doing through all eternity he has and will continue to do.
2. In Philippians 2 we have a window through which we can see that relationship through all eternity. The three Persons of the Trinity have the same goals. They don't compete for first place and are eager to serve each other in perfect harmonious relationship.
B. Representing Christ
1. Jesus gives the reason for unity among believers in John 17:21: "that the world may believe that you have sent me." In other words we have to be a living demonstration of a personal, loving God by treating others in a personal and loving way. This means that the way we relate to others is one of the strongest reflections of the character of our God who seeks to enter into relationship with his creation.
2. If we don't love others, we can't love God (1 John 4:20–21). Others get a picture of God's love through the way we love them.
3. Jesus believed that loving personal relationships are so important that he died to restore our relationship with God the Father.
4. The way we live reveals our true doctrinal beliefs. If you are a cold and distant person who hardly lifts a finger to develop friendships, how can you talk about being in a personal relationship with a God who died to establish a personal relationship with people?
II. The mind (or attitude) for our relationships (vv. 4–5)
A. Valuing the interests and needs of others
1. Christ's attitude (v. 5)
a. This attitude should be ours.
b. This attitude will take every day of our lives to develop.
2. Every human is of infinite worth, made in the image of God. We treat valuable possessions with great care but often abuse people.

   a. Scripture says that the people who surround us are priceless because they carry the image of God.
   b. Jesus says in Matthew 5:22 that calling a person a fool is abuse that is akin to murder.
B. The new attitude in daily life
   1. To deface the image of God by mistreating another person is to insult God who has created him or her.
   2. To love others is honoring to God.
      a. When we love even our enemies, we are living in the revolutionized lifestyle of gospel relationship (Luke 6:32–36).
      b. The breathtaking beauty of our relationships makes the world aware that Jesus Christ is the Savior (John 17:21).
      c. Through our relationships with each other the world sees that we are authentic disciples of Jesus Christ (John 13:34–35).
   3. All relationships are transformed by the power and the reality of the gospel. Believers treat everyone with high esteem. The salesclerk, the cashier, the gas station attendant, the paperboy or papergirl are all highly valued and honored by believers.
III. The method for our relationships
   A. Characteristics of relationships in Christ
      1. "We are like minded" (v. 2).
      2. "We are free from selfish ambition" (v. 3).
      3. We can say, "I'm sorry." It has been said the five most difficult words to say in the English language are, "I'm sorry. I was wrong."
   B. Christ puts high value on Christians being in right relationship with each other
      1. Example 1: If you are at the altar and realize that your relationships are not right, leave your gift and go and reconcile your relationships (Matt. 5:23–24).
      2. Example 2: If you have been offended by someone, you must take the initiative and go to the person (Matt. 18:15). The Christian ideal would be that you would meet as each comes to be reconciled to the other.
   C. Objections to living in right relationships
      1. "Can't I just say I'm sorry to God?" Without a willingness to take the trouble to restore the relationship can you really say that you are sorry?
      2. "This is humiliating." Jesus again has provided us an example by taking on pain and shame to restore our broken relationship with God. This is the attitude that Christ calls us to express in our concern to redeem our relationships.
      3. "It wasn't my fault anyway." This is the most prevalent excuse for Christians living in unreconciled relationships. The answer to this objection is found in Matthew 5:39: "If someone strikes you on the right cheek, turn to him the other also." Faultfinding is usually unproductive—take the first step forward in reconciling conflict-ridden relationships.
      4. "How many times must I forgive?" This was the question that Peter asked in Matthew 18:21. He had hoped seven times would be sufficient. Jesus responded, "Seventy-seven times." Remembering that God has forgiven all our sins should motivate us not to withhold forgiveness from a brother or sister in Christ.
   D. The power of the gospel transforms relationships because it transforms you
      1. As Christians we live to bring praise and honor to Jesus Christ. "Do nothing out of selfish ambition or vain conceit, but in humility consider others better than yourselves. Each of you should look not only to your own interests, but also to the interests of others" (Phil. 2:3–4).
      2. Often conflict in our relationships, caused by hurt feelings or bruised egos, is a symptom of the underlying problem of pride.

3. Our new lifestyle puts Christ in first place then considers the needs of others before our own.

Characteristic 6: Servant-Leadership Development

The healthy church identifies and develops individuals whom God has called and given the gift of leadership and challenges them to be servant-leaders.

Sermon Title: Seven Characteristics of a Shepherd's Heart

Sermon Text: John 10:1–21

Jesus is the wonderful shepherd/pastor. All of Jesus' listeners were very familiar with Psalm 23: "The Lord is my shepherd." Our word for *pastor* comes from the word meaning "shepherd." In John 10 Jesus describes himself as the good shepherd.

In biblical times people understood the characteristics of a shepherd that are underscored in Psalm 23: provision, direction, defense, correction, and protection. Sheep without a shepherd were helpless, wandering, defenseless animals. In John 10 Jesus teaches us about the characteristics of a shepherd's heart.

I. He calls his sheep by name (v. 3)
   A. Personal concern of the Savior for each of his sheep
   B. You are called by name and known personally
      1. A contemporary praise song says it well, "I have a Maker. He knows my name."
      2. The Savior's personal concern for his sheep is a comfort to us who live in a day when we are identified by cards, numbers, and codes.
   C. The Savior's personal concern is a mark of his love
      1. He does not see you as a problem or an illness but as a person he loves.

2. The great shepherd knows his sheep and knows them well. He knows all of the little things about them.
   D. Responding to the shepherd's call
      The greatest encouragement that any pastor knows in the local church is the story of changed lives as people have met the Savior and been transformed.
II. He goes ahead of them and his sheep follow him (v. 4)
   A. Not a leadership model of a drill sergeant yelling commands at new recruits in boot camp
   B. An example to the sheep of leadership
   C. An example of love
      In John 13 Jesus takes the towel and basin and washes the feet of his disciples. John 13:1 says, "He now showed them the full extent of his love."
   D. Jesus' invitation to his disciples
      1. "I have called you to be with me."
      2. Following Christ is an invitation to a new way of life and ministry lifestyle.
      3. Jesus leads the way and his sheep follow him. He gives his sheep himself, not an overhead illustration, not a book, not a lecture but himself as a living example.
   E. Are we good examples to follow?
      What kind of people will your followers become? Suspicious, critical, manipulative, and controlling or loving, encouraging, joyful, and supportive?
III. He finds food for them (v. 9)
   A. Jesus Christ as the perfect shepherd feeds the sheep
   B. Christians are fed spiritually as they experience and encounter the presence of God
      1. They grow.
      2. This is how their character is shaped.
   C. The nourishment of small groups
   D. The need for a balanced diet
      1. Inward growth is growing to be more like Jesus.
      2. Outward growth is in how we respond to God through worship and praise.

3. Outward growth is also seen in outreach to the lost and hurting world all around us.

E. The exercise of the spiritual disciplines

IV. He is willing to lay down his life (v. 11)

A. Christ is a voluntary sacrifice
1. He is not a martyr.
2. He willingly offered himself.

B. We too must count the cost
1. This is part of Jesus' invitation to follow him.
2. To find true life involves death to self.
a. Are you willing to be criticized . . . lay down your life?
b. You won't make everybody happy . . . lay down your life.
c. You will get your feelings hurt . . . lay down your life.
d. You will lose time . . . lay down your life.
e. You will lose money . . . lay down your life.
3. It must be done without complaint, grumbling, or whining.

V. The good shepherd is not like the hired man (v. 12)

A. The good shepherd fights our battles
1. He watches for the enemy.
2. The hired hand runs away.
3. The good shepherd protects us from the enemy.

B. Spiritual warfare is inevitable for those who have a shepherd's heart
Every step forward in the kingdom of God will be accompanied by spiritual opposition and spiritual warfare. The true shepherd is courageous and vigilant. He "sees the wolf coming."

VI. The shepherd cares for the sheep (v. 13)

A. A true shepherd is revealed in love, tenderness, gentleness, and kindness
"People don't care how much you know until they know how much you care" (E. V. Hill).

B. God's love is unconditional, unchanging, and unfailing
1. If God's love were based on your goodness, worthiness, or works, then you could lose his love.

2. God loves you because he loves you; his love is the reason in itself.

C. How to have a shepherd's love
1. You can love others only as you are first filled with God's love.
2. Having received his love, you have a sufficient supply of love to give to everyone he sends to you each day.

VII. The shepherd knows his sheep (v. 14)

A. Intimacy between the shepherd and the sheep

B. Following Christ involves total commitment
1. This is an all or nothing at all relationship.
2. Jesus says, "I tell you the truth, unless you eat the flesh of the Son of Man and drink his blood, you have no life in you" (John 6:53).

C. The invitation to intimacy with the Savior is given again in Revelation 3:20 "Here I am! I stand at the door and knock. If anyone hears my voice and opens the door, I will come in and eat with him, and he with me."

Characteristic 7: An Outward Focus

The healthy church places high priority on communicating the truth of Jesus and demonstrating the love of Jesus to those outside the faith.

Sermon Text: Luke 15

The catalogue of complaints and the chorus of criticisms directed at Jesus Christ by the Pharisees included many accusations. He was called a Sabbath breaker, a glutton and wine drinker, and a friend of sinners. Luke 15:2 reads, "This man welcomes sinners and eats with them." Jesus responds to this contempt by telling three stories about a lost sheep, a lost coin, and a lost son.

I. Lost Sheep

A. Sheep are notoriously stupid animals
Today someone might be called a "turkey" if they behaved in a foolish way. Sheep are careless and foolish. They easily become lost. And once separated

from the flock and the shepherd they wander farther and farther away. Domesticated dogs and cats may wander all over the neighborhood but usually in due time will return home once again. Cows will graze in the pasture but will in due time return home once again. Not so with sheep. Contrary to the poem you learned as a child: "Little Bo Peep has lost her sheep and doesn't know where to find them. Leave them alone and they'll come home, wagging their tails behind them." The truth is sheep would never come home. They would wander farther and farther away from home if left to their own devices.

B. Sheep desperately need a shepherd
   1. The prophet Isaiah says this is something of the story of humanity: "We all, like sheep, have gone astray" (Isa. 53:6).
   2. It is the good shepherd, Jesus Christ, who has come to seek and save the lost.

C. There is celebration when the sheep is found
   1. In verse 6 all of the friends and neighbors are invited to join this celebration.
   2. "There will be more rejoicing in heaven over one sinner who repents than over ninety-nine righteous persons who do not need to repent" (v. 7).

II. The Lost Coin
A. The coin is lost through carelessness
   1. Some people are like sheep and are lost through stupidity.
   2. Money cannot lose itself. It must be lost through carelessness. A coin is not stupid and it does not wander.

B. We all lose things

C. The woman finds the coin after a complete and thorough search
There is a great celebration: "And when she finds it, she calls her friends and neighbors together and says, 'Rejoice with me; I have found my lost coin'" (v. 9).

D. Some people have been lost through the carelessness of others
   1. The words, deeds, actions, and examples of other people influence those who are lost.
   2. The Pharisees paraded their religious behaviors in the community, praying on street corners and in marketplaces, yet they financially oppressed the poor, found excuses and loopholes when it came to helping those who were in need.
   3. We value things and not people, forgetting that every encounter with an individual moves that friend either closer to God or closer to a destiny of destruction.

III. The Lost Son
A. The boy chooses to be lost
   1. He carefully premeditates his escape from home.
     a. He demands his inheritance even before his father's death.
     b. He takes his share of the inheritance and goes off to a distant country full of high hopes.
   2. The boy finds only disappointment and finally "hits bottom."

B. The boy comes to his senses
In his desperation, his heart turns toward home: "I will . . . go back to my father and say to him, 'Father, I have sinned against heaven and against you. I am no longer worthy to be called your son; make me like one of your hired men'" (vv. 18–19).

C. The father waits for the son
   1. The reunion: "When he was still a long way off, his father saw him and was filled with compassion for him; he ran to his son, threw his arms around him and kissed him."
   2. The boy's speech of confession is quickly interrupted by the father who calls to the servants: "Quick! Bring the best robe and put it on him. Put a ring on his finger and sandals on his feet" (v. 22).

a. The robe is the garment of a son and not a beggar.

b. The ring identifies this boy as a true son of his father.

c. The sandals would soon be needed for celebration, for a great party will be held with music and dancing.

D. This story is the story of every lost son It is the story of every prodigal who finds his way home to his father's heart.

IV. The other lost son

Now there is also an older brother in the story and there is obvious sibling rivalry. The older brother is intelligent, industrious, diligent, frugal, and very proud of himself.

A. The older brother returns home

1. In his anger, stubbornness, and sulkiness he refuses to go into the party.

2. The inner attitude of the heart will reveal itself sooner or later in some unguarded moment, in some careless word.

B. The older brother's true nature

1. Disrespect to his father

2. Cruel disregard for his younger brother

C. A portrait of the Pharisees

1. Just beneath the religious veneer is a heart of arrogance and contempt for the lost, not compassion.

2. The lost older brother is just as lost as the prodigal younger brother.

V. Lost people really matter to God

A. Three stories teach the same principle

B. There is celebration when the lost is found

When lost people turn to the Father, he welcomes them with open arms of love and receives them in the divine embrace of salvation.

Characteristic 8: Wise Administration and Accountability

The healthy church utilizes appropriate facilities, equipment, and systems to provide maximum support for the growth and development of its ministries.

Sermon Text: Acts 6:1–7

The Book of Acts tells the story of the apostolic church, a church of dynamic spiritual power where remarkable signs, wonders, and miracles were daily occurrences. The Book of Acts also tells the difficulties of the early church—the problems of persecution and the problems with people, hypocrisy, and lying. In Acts 6 there is complaining and murmuring among the members of the early church.

I. The problem emerges

A. The complaint

The complaint is that the Greek widows felt that they were being treated unfairly and that the Hebrew widows were receiving preferential treatment. Both groups were Jewish believers who had come to faith in Christ. But one group was Greek speaking.

It seems hard to believe sometimes that even in the early church there was complaining and there were problems. We tend to idealize the early church and think that it was a place where "never was heard a discouraging word and the skies were not cloudy all day."

B. An important principle

We learn in this passage that internal problems and conflict in the church do not mean that the church is unhealthy or on the brink of division. The passage should encourage believers in healthy churches to know that even the early church had problems. Here we find the apostles trying to find a solution to the real problems of real people.

C. Every church has problems

The problems of life and growth are to be preferred every time to the problems of death and decay. Healthy churches will have problems and will experience conflict. But these problems and conflicts when handled and managed with wisdom can result in greater usefulness and blessing for the people of God.

II. The problem is resolved

A. In verse 3 the problem is resolved by an expansion of the base of ministry leaders

The apostles have discerned that a greater base of ministry leaders is needed to care for the issues that are at the heart of this problem. The apostles also realize that if they try to meet these needs themselves, their own time for preaching, teaching, and prayer will be diminished.

B. All seven of the first deacons appear to be Greek believers

Apparently the apostles were anxious to correct the appearance of favoritism and in making these appointments they demonstrate that true love governs all relationships within the church.

III. Lessons to learn today

A. Suspicion of the motives of church leaders can cause trouble in the church today

Why was one person appointed, selected, assigned to a particular job? Suspicion, if not dealt with, can result in bitterness, hurt feelings, unforgiveness, and anger.

B. Everyone is insecure in some place deep within

Even people who enjoy great acceptance within the church body can experience times of vulnerability. We might feel overlooked or that someone simply does not like us.

C. The importance of knowing that you are accepted

It is important for believers to rest in the fact that we have been accepted by God and enjoy the love that he has so generously and unconditionally given to us. Real love and acceptance begins with the knowledge that we are loved by God.

IV. The church restructures its ministry

A. God calls all his people to ministry and gives them gifts to use to build up the church

B. God calls different people to different ministries

The apostles recognized this in calling out the seven deacons who had been selected to serve the needs of God's people. The apostles had their ministry of preaching, teaching, and prayer. The deacons had their ministry of serving the needs of the people of God in practical acts of mercy. Both ministries served people but in different ways.

C. The results of the early church restructuring and reorganization

Verse 7 tells us that the Word spreads and increases in the growing apostolic church. The number of believers increases rapidly. The bottleneck and gridlock in the early church has been resolved by expanding the base of ministry leaders. The apostles have released themselves to do the ministry that God has given to them in preaching, teaching, and prayer. This restructuring and reorganization of ministry has a profound impact on the leadership of Israel, and many priests come to a living faith in Jesus Christ.

V. Wise administration and accountability

A. The apostles did not diverge from their mission to wait on tables

They solved the problem by appointing others to meaningful ministry and held them accountable to fulfill their task.

B. The plan was orchestrated by the Holy Spirit and as a result the impact on the early church was powerful

C. Constructing plans without full reliance on God will most certainly pull you off mission and into activities counterproductive to God's call

Administrate wisely and hold one another accountable to fulfill *his* mission.

Characteristic 9: Networking with the Body of Christ

The healthy church reaches out to others in the body of Christ for collaboration, resource sharing, learning opportunities, and united celebrations of worship.

Sermon Text: Psalm 133

It is not at all unusual to meet someone who proclaims that they are a Christian although they have no use for the local church. It is no more God's intention for Christians to be Christians alone than for married people to be alone. The idea of being a Christian all by yourself is certainly not God's idea. First Corinthians 12:13 says, "For we were all baptized by one Spirit into one body . . . and we were all given the one Spirit to drink."

When you become a Christian you become part of that spiritual body of Jesus Christ. From the moment you confess Christ as Lord and Savior, you are part of the Christian church, not a building but a living body of believers.

No Christian is an only child. God never makes private salvation deals with people. Salvation is personal and it is intimate but it is never exclusive. When you become a Christian you join a family and have brothers and sisters who share your relationship with God as Father.

I. Unity and community
   A. What the family of God is supposed to be
   B. Jesus and the twelve disciples lived together in unity and community
   C. The New Testament church
      1. Emerged on the Day of Pentecost.
      2. "They were all together in one place" (Acts 2:1).
      3. When some New Testament Christians stopped attending worship and fellowship, they were exhorted in Hebrews 10:25 to not stop meeting together and encouraging one another.
   D. The beauty of the church
      The great commandment given by the Savior to love God with all your heart, soul, strength, and mind is combined with the command to love your neighbor as yourself (Matt. 22:37–39). The beauty of the church is the beauty of God's people living together in unity and community.
   E. A singing community
      1. Psalm 133 was a travelers' song, sung by worshipers on their pilgrimage to Jerusalem.
      2. All of the singers shared one common purpose, one common path, and one common goal.
II. Complications and blessings of community
   A. "Brothers"
      1. Many of us have had firsthand experience in growing up with brothers.
      2. Brothers fight, and sisters fight. Most biblical families seem to be dysfunctional families.
         a. Cain and Abel, a brother's murder.
         b. Joseph and his brothers, a kidnapping.
         c. Even Jesus was misunderstood by his own brothers.
   B. "Brothers live together in unity"
      1. God's design is for his people to live together in unity.
      2. Unity is expressed in worship, fellowship, and outreach.
      3. It is our visible unity that Jesus says is the proof that we are authentic disciples because we "love one another" (John 13:35).
      4. This characteristic love must be seen in our conversation, teamwork, and relationships so that the watching world will recognize true disciples of Jesus Christ.
III. Two symbols of unity: oil and dew
   A. Precious oil
      "It is like precious oil poured on the head, running down on the beard, running down on Aaron's beard, down upon the collar of his robes."
      1. This picture comes from Exodus 29 where the instructions are given for the ordination of Aaron and other priests. Exodus 29:7, 9 "Take the anointing oil and anoint him by pouring it on his head. . . . In this way you shall ordain Aaron and his sons."
      2. Oil throughout Scripture is used as a symbol of the Holy Spirit, a sign of God's presence.

3. The anointing oil was fragrant, giving a pleasant aroma.
4. Anointing oil was refreshing and would soften the skin.
5. Anointing oil would shine, reminding one of the radiance of God's presence among his people.
6. Anointing oil consecrated an individual and identified him as a priest chosen by God.

B. Dew
   "It is as if the dew of Hermon were falling on Mount Zion" (v. 3).
   1. Morning dew is characteristic of a new day, a new time of refreshing, a reminder that God's mercies are new every morning.
   2. Mt. Hermon is mentioned because it is the highest mountain in that region. The morning dew would be drenching, heavy dew.
   3. This heavy dew falling on Mt. Zion would make it richly fruitful. God's people dwelling together in unity would make their community richly fruitful.
   4. This dew, which falls from heaven, would sustain the life of the people of God, physically, just as God himself sustains the life of his people spiritually. Spiritual unity brings growth with excitement and anticipation in the miracle of spiritual unity and growth. God accomplishes what would appear to be impossible to human beings.
   5. When the dew of heaven falls on God's people, they accomplish great things in the kingdom. God uses ordinary people to accomplish extraordinary results.

C. Separating and sanctifying
   Both symbols, oil and dew, soak and saturate God's people in spiritual unity, separating and sanctifying them as God's people.

IV. The blessing of unity
   A. God bestows his blessing
      "For there the LORD bestows his blessing, even life forevermore" (v. 3). God commands his blessing on unity when believers celebrate unity, live in unity, and value unity. The ultimate result of believers living in unity is the picture of believers enjoying life everlasting in heaven.
   B. Ultimate fulfillment in heaven
      All of our unity that gives deepest joy, fullest friendship, and delight in shared experiences is only a hint of the everlasting joy in store for those who receive God's commanded blessing on unity, life forevermore.

Characteristic 10: Stewardship and Generosity

The healthy church teaches its members that they are stewards of their God-given resources and challenges them to be sacrificially generous in sharing with others.

Sermon Text: 2 Corinthians 8–9

Disaster struck Jerusalem in the form of an agricultural famine. This caused the Christians in Jerusalem extreme hardship, suffering, and hunger.

The apostle Paul, responding to this disaster, called on the Gentile churches to come to the relief of their Jewish Christian brothers and sisters. The apostle intended this to be a beautiful way to demonstrate the unity of the body of Christ and break down the old walls between Jews and Gentiles.

Wherever Paul went, he told about the need in Jerusalem. When he mentioned this disaster to the Macedonian churches, their response was tremendous. The churches in Macedonia were poor and suffering and yet they were united in great generosity. The church in Corinth was wealthy and comfortable and yet divided and selfish. Paul outlines for the Corinthians seven principles of Christian stewardship.

I. Principle 1: True grace originates with God

"We want you to know about the grace that God has given the Macedonian churches" (2 Cor. 8:1).
A. We respond to God's generosity
We respond in giving because we have first received abundantly of the grace and generosity of God himself.
B. The Macedonians gave
1. They gave despite their own suffering, "severe trial," and "extreme poverty" (v. 2).
2. They were motivated by the grace of God to generous giving.
3. The Macedonians were moved with compassion because they understood the pain of their own extreme poverty.
II. Principle 2: Christian giving is a privilege
"They urgently pleaded with us for the privilege of sharing in this service to the saints" (v. 4).
A. Paul may have been reluctant
Paul probably was reluctant to tell the Macedonians about the need in Jerusalem because he thought they could not respond in their difficult circumstances.
B. The Macedonians wanted to share
1. They pleaded for the privilege of sharing with the believers in Jerusalem.
2. They had their priorities and values in the right place.
III. Principle 3: Give yourself first
"They gave themselves first to the Lord and then to us in keeping with God's will" (v. 5).
A. Everything we have belongs to God
B. You cannot serve both God and money
1. No one can be completely obedient to both masters.
2. Jesus taught this truth in his encounter with the rich young ruler who refused to follow Christ, choosing his wealth instead.
3. Jesus taught this truth in the story of the rich farmer who chose to build bigger barns rather than share his excessive wealth.
IV. Principle 4: Christian giving is a proof of true love

"I am not commanding you, but I want to test the sincerity of your love by comparing it with the earnestness of others" (v. 8).
A. Actions prove authentic love
B. True Christians are action oriented
1. They back up their claims with their conduct.
2. It is now time for the Corinthians to prove that their love is genuine.
V. Principle 5: Jesus Christ is our example in giving
"For you know the grace of our Lord Jesus Christ, that though he was rich, yet for your sakes he became poor, so that you through his poverty might become rich" (v. 9).
A. Paul's theme
B. Grace is the foundation of giving
C. Christ's life of grace
1. Christ was rich in the glory of heaven and yet he chose to humble himself and become poor.
2. Christ on earth borrowed everything, had nothing of his own, was born in a stable, was given food and clothing, borrowed a coin for an illustration, borrowed a donkey to enter Jerusalem, borrowed a tomb of Joseph of Arimathea for three days.
VI. Principle 6: Give what you can
"According to your means" (v. 11).
A. God is not unreasonable
B. The Corinthians are reminded of their commitment (vv. 10–12)
1. No collection had been taken.
2. They could do as well as the Macedonians.
C. The poor often give
1. The poorest financially often are the most generous in giving.
2. Jesus celebrates the generosity of the widow in Luke 21:4.
VII. Principle 7: The principle of equality of response (vv. 13–15)
A. A time for generosity
1. When the need exists.
2. We will receive when we are in need.
B. Identifying with those in need
1. The principle of equality says that we can never say what's mine is mine as

long as there is a brother who is in need. We must say, if my brother hurts, then I hurt.

2. In verse 15 Paul refers to Exodus 16:18, "He who gathered much did not have too much, and he who gathered little did not have too little."

3. When the manna fell in the wilderness, all of God's people were fed. The record in Scripture tells that when the people received God's provision they shared with those who were in need.

4. It is God's design that generous giving, motivated by the grace we have so generously received from God, will provide for all the needs we encounter.

Appendix C

Healthy Church Facilitation

A case study written by Bob Ludwig

Seaside Community Church, Seaside, Rhode Island

The assessment process began for Seaside Community Church when Sam Mitchell, chair of the deacons, phoned Bob Ludwig, director of healthy church facilitation at Vision New England. Sam sought details concerning the assessment process and how it might work in his church. Bob answered his questions, summarizing the process. He later explained the process to Joe Mason, the pastor of Seaside. When Sam and the pastor reported their findings to the board of deacons, the board decided to proceed with the healthy church assessment, using Bob as the facilitator. Then a contract between Seaside Community Church and Vision New England was drawn up, specifying the purpose of the self-assessment, the process that would be followed, the length of time required, and the fee.

Before the Planning Task Force met for their first session with Bob Ludwig, they filled out the self-assessment instrument and rated their church on the Ten Characteristics of a Healthy Church. They also asked the congregation to fill out the short version of the self-assessment and compiled the results.

Session One

After reviewing the results of the self-assessment, Bob made the following observations to the leadership team:

- The average score from the congregation was always higher than that from the Planning Task Force. There appear to be no "pockets of discontent" in the pew.
- The ordering of the strengths and weaknesses was reasonably similar, but not identical, for both the Planning Task Force and the congregation.
- None of the ten characteristics was rated very low; the lowest rating for the Planning Task Force was 2.9, a characteristic the congregation rated at 3.8.
- This is a very good "report card."
- The three greatest strengths, as identified by the Task Force and the congregation, were God-Exalting Worship, God's Empowering Presence, and Wise Administration and Accountability.
- The three greatest weaknesses, as identified by the Task Force and the congregation, were Spiritual Disciplines, Servant-Leadership Development, and an Outward Focus.
- The job of the Planning Task Force is to make a healthy church even healthier.

After reviewing the ratings on all ten characteristics, Bob led the group in brainstorming for the future. Before brainstorming, Bob reminded them of the following brainstorming guidelines:

1. No idea is a bad idea.
2. Disagreement is okay.
3. No one person dominates the conversation.
4. Comments should be concise.
5. Build on what others suggest.
6. Be creative—think outside the box.

For the remainder of session one, the Planning Task Force brainstormed about the first three characteristics one-by-one by answering the following question:

What's our dream for this church in these characteristics two years from now?

All ideas were captured on a flip chart for future reference.

Sessions Two and Three

In sessions two and three the same question was asked for characteristics four through ten.

At the conclusion of session three, the Planning Task Force had generated many ideas on how Seaside Community Church could be strengthened in each of the ten characteristics during the next two years. The ideas were not sorted or prioritized but were used as the basis for later discussion on ministry goals for the future.

Then Bob gave them an assignment to complete for the next session. Each member of the Task Force was asked to write out the answer to the following questions and bring them to the next session:

1. If you were asked by an unchurched neighbor what's good about your church, what three things would you say?
2. If you could make three significant changes in your church over the next two years, what would they be?

Session Four

When the Task Force met again and shared their responses to the two questions, they discovered certain common themes. These themes

were categorized with the following result. The strengths of Seaside Community Church are:

1. Welcoming, warm, caring, loving people
2. Biblically based teaching
3. God's presence felt, especially in worship
4. Diverse ministries
5. Safe environment for people who are searching for God
6. People who love and sense God in practical ways

The categories where changes were needed are:

1. Prayer
2. Growing deeper in Christ
3. Outreach
4. Developing and implementing a long-range growth plan
5. Removing time constraints in worship

Session Five

In session five the Task Force began the process of turning the areas identified for church improvement into future ministry goals. The aim was to develop SMART goals for the ideas generated in session four. The following goals were developed as a first step but they needed further refinement to meet the SMART goals criteria.

Prayer

- Show our reliance on God by being committed to praying individually and corporately for all members, visitors, children, ministries, decisions, pastors, and leaders
- Emphasize intercessory prayer for worship
- Spend more time in prayer in committee meetings and business meetings

Growing Deeper in Christ

- Be more generous with our time, abilities, money, and other resources
- Involve more church members in spiritual growth

- Grow through personal study and application of the Bible as well as through Sunday school and small-group Bible studies

Outreach

- Intentional outreach to teenagers
- Greater outreach to the elderly
- Outreach to the alienated who are turned off and tuned out
- More concerted effort to connect with people who are missing
- Develop missions team to educate, activate, and coordinate outreach

Long-Range Growth Plan

- Develop a plan to minister to more people in the community
- Develop a parking plan
- Develop more Sunday school space
- Develop more sanctuary space
- Have multiple worship services

Removing Time Constraints in Worship

- Use time effectively for worship and Sunday school
- Be good stewards of resources God has given and develop a comprehensive plan for their use

Session Six

More specifics concerning the goals were discussed in session six. The team asked the pastor, Sam Mitchell, and Bob Ludwig to do the final refinement needed to make them truly SMART goals. As these three people worked on the goals, they kept in mind the size of the congregation and its resources so as to develop goals that were doable. They also reviewed the church's statement of faith, its purpose statement, vision statement, motto, and key Scripture verse to be sure the goals they developed were consistent with them.

Here are the final goals as they were approved by the Planning Task Force and the Board of Deacons:

Prayer

1. To strengthen the ministry of the church by concerted, systematic prayer, through establishment of a Prayer Team that will commit itself to praying together weekly for (a) all aspects of the church's ministry; (b) all people within the church in need of prayer; and (c) prayer requests from ministries around the world—with at least 20 people on the Prayer Team by December 2001.
2. To seek God's guidance for all church decisions by gradually increasing the time spent in prayer at committee meetings until all church committees are devoting 33 percent of their time to prayer by December 2002.
3. To strengthen and increase the midweek prayer service of the church and to increase average weekly attendance to 15 people by December 2001.
4. To engage people in urgent prayer on the spur of the moment anytime during the week, by strengthening and rejuvenating the prayer chain that will gradually increase its involvement until it includes at least 25 percent of all church members by December 2002.
5. To create two or three new and engaging opportunities for prayer during 2002 to encourage church members and attendees to engage in meaningful prayer in different formats, such as prayer walks with two or three people, 24-hour prayer vigils two or three times each year, prayer oases, concerts of prayer and praise, in addition to the above, regular, ongoing prayer opportunities.

Growing Deeper in Christ

1. To strengthen individuals' personal walk with Christ through increased participation in community building groups that include Bible study, prayer, caring for one another, and personal accountability for spiritual growth so that 35 percent of all church members are involved in such groups by December 2001 and 45 percent

of church members are participating by December 2002.

2. To assist each church member to identify his or her spiritual gifts and to challenge each person to utilize his or her spiritual gifts in one or two church ministries in a regular, ongoing basis by December 2002.

3. To increase the generosity of church members who contribute financially for kingdom purposes such that 50 percent of all members will practice disciplined giving and move toward tithing by December 2002.

4. To develop new and enhanced ministries that focus on the special needs of women, children, the elderly, and families. A written plan to address this will be developed by June 2002.

Outreach

1. To develop a systematic but caring way, that will be implemented by May 2001, to reach out to and care for (a) church visitors and (b) regular attendees who are absent from the Sunday worship services.

2. To increase attendance by non-Christians at First Saturdays by having more members invite their non-Christian friends.

3. To enhance and enlarge the outreach efforts of the church to (a) teenagers, by September 2001; (b) the elderly, by January 2002; and (c) pre-teenage children, by September 2002.

4. To intentionally reach out to more people in our community who do not know Christ, beginning in the fall of 2001, through planning and implementing three or four creative evangelistic events each ministry year. These outreach activities could be a part of larger community events such as the Greater Seaside Thanksgiving Celebration, the Clam Festival, and the Christmas Fair or could be events sponsored solely by the church such as Men's Breakfasts, activities for the elderly, etc.

5. To evangelize inquiring adults by sponsoring one APLHA (a small-group ministry) class each year.

6. To create an Evangelism and Missions Team that will plan and coordinate all outreach activities of the church and will motivate members and attendees to participate by September 2001.

Wider in Vision

1. To enable the church to minister to even more people in the interim future (September 2001–August 2002) as well as in the long-term future (September 2002 and beyond), by forming a Future Growth Task Force by February 2001 that will identify options, conduct research, evaluate the pros and cons of alternative plans, and make action recommendations to the congregation for supporting a vital ministry to many more people.

2. The issues that will be investigated by the Future Growth Task Force would include, but not be limited to, use of multiple worship services, remote parking lots, reconfiguration of the current structure, the potential addition of a balcony in the sanctuary, the alternative uses of the recent bequest to provide growth opportunities for this congregation or investment in other ministries or both.

Implementation and Monitoring of Progress

Each SMART goal was assigned to a ministry team, which will develop an action plan that lists the steps that must occur to accomplish the goal. Each action plan will answer the following questions:

Who? (Who will do it?)
What? (What will be done?)
When? (When will it be accomplished?)
Resources? (What resources are needed?)

Each action plan will be approved by the Board of Deacons. Then, every three months, the deacons will devote one meeting to confer with the chairpersons of each ministry assigned a goal to:

- Review progress on achieving the goal
- Affirm progress made

- Brainstorm with the chairperson on ways to overcome obstacles
- Adjust goals, if appropriate
- Pray for each ministry

Seaside Community Church anticipates spiritual and numerical growth as a result of implementing the SMART goals they have developed.

Additional Healthy Church Resources and Training Opportunities

Publications

Becoming a Healthy Church in English (Baker, 1999) and Korean (Agape, 2000), soon to be published in Spanish and Russian

Ten Characteristics of a Healthy Church summary booklets in English, Spanish, Korean, soon to be published in Portuguese, Russian, and French

Short versions of Assessment Tools with Excel Tabulation Spreadsheet Software

• Leadership Team Assessment Tool—short version of section 2 of this workbook, "Time for Dialogue and Assessment," including basic evaluative questions for leadership team to complete

• Congregation Assessment Tool—designed to gain input from members of the congregation to enhance leadershp team discussion as the church proceeds through the healthy church assessment process

• Additional Assessment Questions for Ten Characteristics of a Healthy Church—hundreds of helpful questions for enhancing the leadership team dialogue and assessment process

Future publications

• *Becoming a Healthy Disciple* (Baker, 2002)
• *Becoming a Healthy Team* (Baker, 2002)

Surveys and Reports

"Healthy Church Visits" 14-question survey and reports of 100 interviews

"Church Attitude Survey Reports / Executive Summaries from Congress '97 and '98" Computerized surveys of nearly 2,000 believers at each event

Seminars and Ministries

Healthy Church Leadership Development Seminars

One- or three-day seminars for pastors and church leaders focusing on:

• *Attributes*—Ten Characteristics of a Healthy Church
• *Assessment*—dialogue process for pastors, leaders, congregations
• *Action*—Spirit-directed strategic planning process for local churches

Healthy Church Facilitators/Consultants

Trained pastors available for local church assessment and planning process

Healthy Church Network

Teams of pastors, regional advisors, and Vision New England staff members in partnership with one another for the health of local churches and communities

Pastoral Mentors
  Older, wiser pastors investing in lives of younger pastors for their spiritual, relational, and ministry health
Pastors' Prayer Summits
  Annual summits held for pastors in entire region, as well as sub-regional summits for various cities and states

Services Offered by Vision New England Staff, Ministries, and Programs

Annual Congress for renewal, training, and resource sharing
Annual Equip Conference, focusing on Christian education and church ministry training
Healthy Church Seminars
Women in the Word
Ministry Specific Events

Prison Ministries
50-Plus Care Ministries
Deaf Ministries
Disabilities Ministries
Recovery Ministries

Men's Ministries
Women's Ministries

Family Builders Ministry
Youth Ministry
Children's Ministry Network

Church Leadership Services
Healthy Church Network
Healthy Church Facilitators
Healthy Church Consultants
Church Planting Network
Worship Renewal Ministries
Small-Group Ministries
Pastors Prayer Summits
Pastoral Mentoring
Project One

For information on all of these resources and training opportunities contact Vision New England:

www.VisionNewEngland.com

Vision New England
468 Great Road
Acton, MA 01720
978-929-9800
fax 978-929-9898
Toll free for orders and event registrations
877-734-HOPE

Selected Bibliography

Additional Dialogue, Assessment, and Planning Resources

Anderson, Leith. *Dying for Change.* Minneapolis: Bethany House Publishers, 1990.

Barna, George. *The Power of Vision.* Ventura, Calif.: Regal, 1992.

Bridges, William. *Managing Transitions: Making the Most of Change.* Cambridge, Mass.: Perseus Books, 1991.

Cladis, George. *Leading the Team-Based Church.* San Francisco: Jossey-Bass, 1999.

Collins, James C. *Built to Last.* New York: Harper Business, 1994.

Covey, Stephen R. *First Things First.* New York: Simon and Schuster, 1994.

Easum, William M., and Thomas G. Bandy. *Growing Spiritual Redwoods.* Nashville: Abingdon Press, 1997.

Gladwell, Malcolm. *The Tipping Point.* Boston: Little, Brown, 2000.

Herrington, Jim, Mike Bonem, and James H. Furr. *Leading Congregational Change.* San Francisco: Jossey-Bass, 2000.

Herrington, Jim, Mike Bonem, and James H. Furr. *Leading Congregational Change Workbook.* San Francisco: Jossey-Bass, 2000.

Hesselbein, Francis, Marshall Goldsmith, and Richard Beckhard, eds. *The Organization of the Future.* San Francisco: Jossey-Bass, 1997.

Hunter, Dale, Anne Bailey, and Bill Taylor. *The Art of Facilitation.* Tucson: Fisher Books, 1995.

Hybels, Lynne and Bill. *Rediscovering Church.* Grand Rapids: Zondervan, 1995.

Johnson, Spencer, M.D. *Who Moved My Cheese?* New York: G. P. Putnam's Sons, 1998.

Katzenbach, Jon R. and Douglas K. Smith. *The Wisdom of Teams.* New York: Harper Business, 1993.

Kotter, John P. *Leading Change.* Boston: Harvard Business School Press, 1996.

McIntosh, Gary L. *One Size Doesn't Fit All.* Grand Rapids: Revell, 1999.

Rehnborg, Sarah Jane. *The Starter Kit for Mobilizing Ministry.* Dallas: Leadership Network, 1994.

Rogers, Everett M. *Diffusion of Innovations.* New York: The Free Press, 1995.

Schaller, Lyle E. *The Change Agent.* Nashville: Abingdon Press, 1972.

Schaller, Lyle E. *Getting Things Done.* Nashville: Abingdon Press, 1986.

Southerland, Dan. *Transitioning: Leading Your Church through Change.* Littleton, Colo.: Serendipity House, 1999.

Stern, Gary J. *The Drucker Foundation Self-Assessment Tool: Process Guide.* San Francisco: Jossey-Bass, 1999.

Sweet, Leonard. *Aqua Church.* Loveland, Colo.: Group Publishers, 1999.

Thompson, Robert R. and Gerald R. Thompson. *Organizing for Accountability: How to Avoid Crisis in Your Non-profit Ministry.* Wheaton, Ill.: Harold Shaw, 1991.

Warren, Rick. *The Purpose-Driven Church.* Grand Rapids: Zondervan, 1995.

Yankelovich, Daniel. *The Magic of Dialogue.* New York: Simon and Schuster, 1999.

The Rev. Dr. Stephen A. Macchia has served as president of Vision New England (formerly known as The Evangelistic Association of New England) since March 1989. During his tenure the association moved from rented offices in Boston to its own offices in Acton, attained financial stability, saw participation in its annual Congress more than double, organized the Interdependent Church Network, reorganized its Outreach Ministries, established its first state offices in Connecticut and New Hampshire, and developed the nationally recognized Healthy Church Initiative, with its Ten Characteristics of a Healthy Church. Steve's emphasis on servant leadership and networking have resulted in a growing renewal movement and healthy interchurch cooperation in the region. Before assuming the leadership of Vision New England, Steve spent eleven years in pastoral ministry.

Steve earned the master of divinity and doctor of ministry degrees from Gordon-Conwell Theological Seminary in South Hamilton, Massachusetts. He is currently on the D.Min. teaching team at Gordon-Conwell, and he leads seminars on leadership, church health, team building, family life, and spiritual vitality.

Steve and Ruth Macchia have two children, Nathan and Rebekah, and make their home in Lexington, Massachusetts.

Vision New England was founded in 1887 as the Evangelistic Association of New England. Today it is a formidable force in the region, serving as a church-based renewal ministry designed to bring together five thousand congregations from eighty denominations. The primary focus of this unique regional ministry is the spiritual renewal of New England. They accomplish this vision by fostering unprecedented unity within the body of Christ, resourcing pastors and ministry leaders in their development of healthy churches in every community of the region, and training disciples in the evangelistic mission of the church. Through the effective proclamation of the gospel of Jesus Christ, thousands of lives have been transformed by the power of God.

For additional information on Vision New England, contact:

www.VisionNewEngland.com
Vision New England
468 Great Road
Acton, MA 01720
978-929-9800
978-929-9898 (fax)
Toll free for orders and registrations 877-734-HOPE